WITHDRAWN

MAXWELL ANDERSON: *The Playwright As Prophet*

Plays by
Maxwell Anderson

1923	White Desert
1924	What Price Glory
1924	Sea Wife
1925	Outside Looking In
1925	First Flight
1925	The Buccaneer
1927	Saturday's Children
1928	Gods of the Lightning
1929	Gypsy
1930	Elizabeth the Queen
1932	Night Over Taos
1933	Both Your Houses
1933	Mary of Scotland
1934	Valley Forge
1935	Winterset
1936	The Wingless Victory
1937	The Masque of Kings
1937	High Tor
1937	The Star Wagon
1938	Knickerbocker Holiday
1938	Second Overture
1939	Key Largo
1940	Journey to Jerusalem
1941	Candle in the Wind
1942	The Eve of St. Mark
1944	Storm Operation
1946	Joan Of Lorraine
1946	Truckline Cafe
1948	Anne of the Thousand Days
1949	Lost in the Stars
1951	Barefoot in Athens
1954	Bad Seed

MAXWELL ANDERSON

The Playwright As Prophet

MABEL DRISCOLL BAILEY

ABELARD-SCHUMAN
London and New York

Contents

Acknowledgments

The author wishes to thank the following: RANDOM HOUSE, INC., for permission to quote from *The American Drama Since 1918* by Joseph Wood Krutch (Copyright 1939 by Random House, Inc.); HARCOURT, BRACE AND COMPANY, INC., for permission to quote from *Selected Essays* by T. S. Eliot, and from *Three American Plays* by Maxwell Anderson and Laurence Stallings; JOHN MASON BROWN, for permission to quote from *Two on the Aisle*, published by W. W. Norton & Company, Inc.; CORNELL UNIVERSITY PRESS, for permission to quote from *'Modernism' in Modern Drama* by Joseph Wood Krutch; LONGMANS, GREEN & CO., INC., for permission to quote from *Gods of the Lightning* by Maxwell Anderson and Harold Hickerson, and from *Elizabeth the Queen* by Maxwell Anderson; WILLIAM SLOANE ASSOCIATES, INC., for permission to quote from the following books by Maxwell Anderson: *Barefoot in Athens* (Copyright 1951 by Maxwell Anderson), *Off Broadway* (Copyright 1947 by Maxwell Anderson), and *Lost in the Stars* (Copyright 1949 by Maxwell Anderson and Kurt Weill; Copyright 1950 by Maxwell Anderson); DODD, MEADE & CO., for permission to quote from *Bad Seed* (Copyright 1955 by Maxwell Anderson); and to ANDERSON HOUSE, for permission to quote from the following plays by Maxwell Anderson: *Winterset* (Copyright 1953 by Anderson House), *Night Over Taos* (Copyright 1932 by Maxwell Anderson), *Mary of Scotland* (Copyright 1933 by Maxwell Anderson), *Valley Forge* (Copyright 1934 by Maxwell Anderson), *The Wingless Victory* (Copyright 1936 by Maxwell Anderson), *The Masque of Kings* (Copyright 1937 by Maxwell Anderson), *High Tor* (Copyright 1937 by Maxwell Anderson), *The Feast of Ortolans* (Copyright 1937 by Maxwell Anderson), *Second Overture* (Copyright 1938 by Maxwell Anderson), *Knickerbocker Holiday* (Copyright 1938 by Maxwell Anderson), *Key Largo* (Copyright 1939 by Maxwell Anderson), *Journey to Jerusalem* (Copyright 1940 by Maxwell Anderson), *Candle in the Wind* (Copyright 1941 by Maxwell Anderson), *Storm Operation* (Copyright 1944 by Maxwell Anderson).

Introduction

When I discovered Maxwell Anderson's *Off Broadway*, some four or five years after its unheralded publication in 1947, I asked myself, and then began asking others, why these essays on playwriting by one of the foremost dramatists of the contemporary theatre failed to set in motion for modern drama the same kind of lively discussion which has been sifting the values of poetry and fiction for the past thirty years. My inquiries have elicited two opinions: Mr. Anderson's dramatic theory is not original, and it applies only to his own practice. It is the first, not the second judgment, which accounts for the general dismissal of *Off Broadway*.

Even if it were true that Mr. Anderson's artistic principles are applicable only to his own kind of writing, that fact would not of itself render them unworthy of serious consideration. No less a person than T. S. Eliot has declared that more is not to be expected of the critical theory of an artist. In the essay "From Poe to

9

Valéry" he says, "No poet, when he writes his own
art poétique, should hope to do much more than explain, rationalize, defend or prepare the way for his
own practice: that is, for writing his own kind of poetry."

But Mr. Anderson had denied, before it was made,
the charge of having a private aesthetic. He believes
that the principles by which he writes are laws of playwriting in general. "I did discover," he says, "that there
were rules of playwriting which could not be broken.
One by one I unearthed them for myself, or dug them
out of the treatises of predecessors. And by and by
some of them began to look like essentials." And he
interrupts the citation of these rules to add the comment,

> When I had once begun to make discoveries of this sort,
> they came thick and fast. And they applied not, as is nat-
> ural to suppose, to extraordinary plays only—to Shake-
> speare and Jonson and the Greeks—but to all plays, and
> to those in our modern repertory as much as any others.[1]

It is apparent from these observations that Maxwell
Anderson makes no claim to originality in his dramatic
theory. He admits that his principles, though he calls
them discoveries, are only rediscoveries. His concern
is not for the new, but for the valid, old or new. And
the validity of an artistic principle cannot be established
by confining the discussion to the theoretical level. It
can only be determined with reference to the author's
artistic product.

That is the task which I have undertaken in writing
this book. I have tested the validity of Maxwell Ander-

son's creative principles by a critical examination of the plays he has produced in accordance with those principles.

Mr. Anderson is at variance with the most distinguished critics among his contemporaries on the central issue of modern criticism, the relation between content and form. His dramatic theory, shared by most of the contemporary playwrights, is simply a reassertion of one of the oldest aesthetic principles on record—that art is a vehicle of communication. And the dramatists, however interested they may have been in new forms, have been frankly concerned with their communications. Indeed, so absorbed have they been in turning the stuff of contemporary life into plays that anyone conversant with conditions and events and the rapid changes of thought over the past forty years might date with a fair degree of accuracy almost any important play produced during that time. Nothing could be more symptomatic of the playwrights' social concern than the attitude expressed by Robert Sherwood in his preface to *Reunion in Vienna*. He apologizes for writing such frothy comedy at such a time—1932. And nothing could seem more irrelevant to the new critics.

/ There can be no adequate treatment of the works of Maxwell Anderson unless one acknowledges at the outset that he regards theme as something embodied in the work of art, not as one device merely of the artistic construct. It is the thing for which the work of art exists. He does not even hesitate to use that word— of all words the most offensive to the new critics— *message*/ At the same time, he gives full recognition, in theory at least, to the claims of form as newly defined by modern critics, declaring that the communications of an artist are different in kind as well as in form from other communications.

> There is always something slightly embarrassing about the public statements of writers and artists, for they should be able to say whatever they have to say in their work, and let it go at that. Moreover, the writer or artist who brings a message of any importance to his generation will find it impossible to reduce that message to a bald statement, or even a clearly scientific statement, because the things an artist has to communicate can be said only in symbols, in the symbols of his art. The work of art is a hieroglyph, and the artist's endeavor is to set forth his vision of the world in a series of picture writings which convey meanings beyond the scope of direct statement.[2]

This opinion is not a mere reiteration of an old critical dogma. It is a traditional concept, to be sure, but sharpened, clarified, in every way rendered more precise by the kind of critical discussion which has taken place in the present century.

It was not easy to find a satisfactory grouping of the plays of Maxwell Anderson. To make the attempt is to be impressed with the richness and variety of his genius. Each play is in some way distinctive, and refuses classification. Such divisions as tragedy and comedy, verse and prose, realism and fantasy, history and journalistic commentary, afford the writer no real breakdown of the subject.

Since each of the plays reflects something of the thinking and a good deal of the mood of the time of its production, there might have been justification, if no greater merit, in discussing them singly in chronological order. But such a method would have precluded a close comparison of certain techniques used for different purposes, and of recurring themes in their different treatments. Since Mr. Anderson's own emphasis is on theme, I have adopted a grouping by themes, or, in some instances, by broad, general subjects. I have discussed at length only a few of the plays, those which seem to me his best, commenting briefly by way of comparison on others as they illustrate success or failure with particular techniques.

Maxwell Anderson was thirty-five years old when he entered the playwriting field from a background of teaching and journalism. He was born at Atlantic, Pennsylvania, December 15, 1888, the son of a Baptist clergyman. He received his education at the various places where his father held pastorates, western Pennsylvania, Ohio, Iowa, and North Dakota, being graduated by the University of North Dakota in 1911. He married Margaret Haskett in the same year, and taught for the next three years in secondary schools in North Dakota and California.

In 1914 he became a student instructor at Leland Stanford University where he took his M.A. degree. After one year as Professor of English at Whittier College in southern California, he went into journalism. The only anecdote out of his first thirty years which has gained currency is that he was discharged from the staff of this Quaker college because of his pacifist convictions. The story, if true, may account in part, at least, for his unfailing perception of the ironic elements in the situations which he has chosen for dramatic treatment.

As a newspaper writer he worked successively on the Grand Forks, North Dakota, *Herald*, the San Francisco *Chronicle*, and the San Francisco *Bulletin*.

While still in California he began contributing poetry to the *New Republic*, and after a brief connection with that magazine as contributor he was invited to join its staff. He went to New York in 1918 and served for the next six years on the editorial staffs of the *New Republic*, the New York *Globe*, and the New York *World*.

In 1923 he wrote his first play, *White Desert*, which was not a theatrical success. Also in 1923 he met Laurence Stallings, at that time writing book reviews for the *World*, and the two began work on *What Price Glory*, which became a great theatrical success. They collaborated on two more plays, *First Flight* and *The Buccaneer*, both produced in 1925, both failures. Then they parted company.

The year 1925 was a remarkably productive one for Mr. Anderson. Besides the two plays already mentioned, he wrote the successful *Outside Looking In*, which was based on Jim Tully's *Beggars of Life*. And he published his only book of verse, *You Who Have Dreams*. He had been one of the founders of a poetry magazine, *Measure*; but after his establishment as a dramatist he directed his poetic impulse to the creation of verse plays.

With the success of *What Price Glory*, Maxwell Anderson gave up newspaper work and has since devoted himself exclusively to playwriting.

---

[1] Maxwell Anderson, *Off Broadway*, William Sloane Associates, Inc., New York, 1947, pp. 24-25.
[2] *Ibid.*, p. 36.

I designed the moral, first,
and to that moral
I invented the fable.—CONGREVE

CHAPTER I

What the Public Expects
of the Playwright

Just as the writers of licentious drama have always excused their moral laxness by protesting that they are obliged to give the public what it wants, Maxwell Anderson accounts for the idealism of his plays by appeal to the same authority: the public demand.

> Analyze any play you please which has survived the test of continued favor, and you will find a moral or a rule of social conduct or a rule of thumb which the race has considered valuable enough to learn and pass along.[1]

> Excellence on the stage is always moral excellence. A struggle on the part of a hero to better his material circumstances is of no interest in a play unless his character is somehow tried in the fire, and unless he comes out of his trial a better man.

> The moral atmosphere of a play must be healthy. An audience will not endure the triumph of evil on the stage.[2]

17

Yet Mr. Anderson affects no superiority to the theatre audiences in their ethical prepossessions. He resorts to none of the tricks by which purveyors of entertainment try to dissociate themselves from the consumers of their productions. And he is entirely untainted by that literary ideal of the godlike aloofness of the creative artist, which so many writers have taken from James Joyce. Aloofness is a strange idea of the godlike to have emerged from a culture in which the highest concept of God is that of incarnation, not detachment but the most absolute involvement with the human adventure.

Mr. Anderson is involved with his audience in the quest for meaning. He sympathizes equally with their skepticism and their faith, with their vulgarity and their exaltation. Once he goes so far as to say that "all faiths are delusions." Yet he does not abandon his faith. He is committed to an unending search. As his theory of art is one of the oldest, so also is his concept of the artist: he regards the poet as prophet.

> The dream of the race is that it may make itself better and wiser than it is, and every great philosopher or artist who has ever appeared among us has turned his face away from what man is toward whatever seems to him most godlike that man may become. Whether the steps proposed are immediate or distant, whether he speaks in the simple parables of the New Testament or the complex musical symbols of Bach and Beethoven, the message is always to the effect that men are not essentially as they are but as they imagine and as they wish to be.[3]

The world we live in is given meaning and dignity, is made

an endurable habitation, by the great spirits who have preceded us and set down their records of nobility or torture or defeat in blazons and symbols which we can understand. I accept these not only as prophecy, but as direct motivation toward some far goal of racial aspiration.[4]

The playwright and the theatre audience are in it together. And what they are in is not a den of iniquity, as our Puritan forefathers believed, but a religious experience, a religious ritual, a religious institution.

Following the list of rules to which I have already alluded in the introduction, Mr. Anderson says,

> I list these technical difficulties because they began eventually to have one meaning for me. They mean that the purpose of the theater is to find, and hold up to our regard, what is admirable in the human race. The theatrical profession may protest as much as it likes, the theologians may protest, and the majority of those who see our plays would probably be amazed to hear it, but the theater is a religious institution devoted entirely to the exaltation of the spirit of man.[5]

Of course, the playwright is not the only contemporary writer interested in meaning in art. "It is the function of all art," says T. S. Eliot, "to give us some perception of an order in life, by imposing an order upon it." The significant word in what Mr. Eliot says is "imposing"—"to give us some perception of an order in life, by *imposing* an order upon it." It is the word which distinguishes the modern concept of meaning in literature from all previous theories. Up to, and even into, the twentieth century the "imitation-of-life" idea

prevailed. It meant different things to different schools
of aesthetics. To the ancients it apparently meant a
representation of all the facts of life so far as they were
understood: of character, of actual or possible situations, of the human predicament, of the behavior of the
gods, and whatever meaning life seemed to have. To
the modern realist it has generally meant a reproduc-
tion of the physical details of a locale, of human behavior as explained by various schools of psychology,
and of the apparent meaninglessness of life. To the
romantics it frequently meant an imitation of the materials of life as separate entities—character, setting,
situation, thoughts, emotions—but not an imitation of
the usual combination of these. The romantic writer
quite deliberately created a new order, to please himself and his readers.

The contemporary writers have likewise created
their own order—to please themselves, if not their
readers—but they believe they have been doing something entirely different from the romantics because their
order is a matter of form only, not of content. The view
as first expressed was extreme, and has been subjected
to some acute criticism. One of the first to protest was
Alfred Kazin, in his book *On Native Grounds*, 1942.
His description of what was going on in the thirties is
accurate as to fact, but it is marred by a tone of exasperation. Chapter fourteen contains such phrases as
"form as a mysterious ultimate value," as an "apothe-
osis in a void," "an indeterminate vision of some secret
ideal," "the last orthodoxy in the absence of all other
orthodoxies." And he accuses the critics of using this

mysterious touchstone, form, quite irresponsibly "in the service of snobbery, eccentricity, rigidity, malice, or plain ignorance."

Mr. Kazin may be pardoned for his immoderate tone. He was writing too close to the time when the strict formal doctrine was carrying all before it. Jacques Barzun's opinion, published seven years later in the *Magazine of Art* (November, 1949), is more judicious: "Although critics often pretend to disregard the subject of a work of art, they respond to it and if repelled attempt to rationalize their impression by impugning the form."

I think this is a fair statement. Many of the contemporary writers unquestionably object to the content of romantic literature, and have allowed that aversion to sharpen the edge of their criticism of the romantics. There is a sense in which both groups of creative writers—the romantics and the modern formalists—have been doing the same thing. They have been creating a world of their own in their art. Whereas the romantics have created design by manipulating circumstances and situations and events to provide an illusion of order with meaning, the modern aesthetes have manipulated myths and metaphors and rhythms and paradoxes and ironies, also to create an illusion of order with meaning. But the contemporary writer feels superior to his predecessors because he has discovered and admits that the illusion of meaning is an illusion. He does not claim any correspondence between the order he has created and anything which might be called objective reality, while he supposes that the romantics believed their created

order to correspond to an order somewhere outside
the poet's imagination.

Many of the romantics did believe they were imi-
tating objective reality. Some of the greatest romantic
writers regarded their visions of order as intuitions of
a cosmic truth. Some believed they discerned in human
affairs a moral order, which they tried to represent
in their art by a process of selection and arrangement,
by a foreshortening of time and a clearing away of
extraneous details. Some looked upon the total construct of the work of art—content and form—as a kind
of miniature of the cosmic order, an image of some
universal truth.

There were, of course, a great many writers, usually
called romantic, who fabricated escape literature knowingly and without making any claims to the contrary.

And there is still another group: those who idealized life, in the belief that dreams are creative, that in
dreams begins reality. And who knows? Perhaps we
are "such stuff as dreams are made on." It is a principal
tenet of the religion which has shaped our culture:
"According to your faith be it done unto you." Professor
Ernest Bernbaum, one of the most sensitive as well as
one of the most profound interpreters of the romantic
writers, has said (whether in print, I do not know,
but at least in his lectures) that he attributes to the
influence of the romantic movement many of the im-
provements in human relations—the modern refinement
in the relations of the sexes, for instance, and the more
humane treatment of children.

I have gone into this matter at some length because

it appears to me that the playwrights of the twentieth century, and particularly Maxwell Anderson, have more in common with the great romantics than they have with their contemporaries. Mr. Anderson's declaration that he regards the utterances of great artists as "direct motivation" is distinctly a romantic idea.

Yet the challenges of the new criticism, like those of modern science and of modern totalitarian politics, have been salutary. They have forced us to think more precisely and to be more honest. To speak of "imposing an order upon life" is the modern writer's way of saying no more than he can say, of saying that faith is merely faith and not certainty. And that needed to be said. Now that it has been said, writers may again adopt and profess a faith without a sense of guilt by association with those who claim to know more than we can know. But the modern man of faith will qualify his utterances.

> A man would be a fool who was certain that his vision of current events was the only right one, who believed that he had come upon the secret of the universe, or who thought he had penetrated, for certain, to the basis of things in literature or anywhere else.[6]

> It may be that there is no absolute up or down in this world, but the race believes that there is, and will not hear of any denial.[7]

This brings us back to the point from which we set out. Mr. Anderson places the responsibility for meaning in drama upon the audience; and he is right to do so. Whatever the artist and the critic may think about the absolute or even the relative unimportance of subject matter, the reader and playgoer desire and expect significant content as well as significant form.

[1] Maxwell Anderson, *Off Broadway*, William Sloane Associates, Inc., New York, 1947, p. 31.
[2] *Ibid.*, p. 26.
[3] *Ibid.*, pp. 39-40.
[4] *Ibid.*, pp. 40-41.
[5] *Ibid.*, pp. 27-28.
[6] *Ibid.*, p. 20.
[7] *Ibid.*, p. 63.

CHAPTER II

The Theme Play
in Miniature

The two one-act plays which Maxwell Anderson wrote
for radio when he was at the height of his creative
power (1937), *Second Overture* and *The Feast of
Ortolans,* furnish an almost too perfect demonstration
of the successful and unsuccessful handling of the theme
play, or drama of ideas. William Archer in his book
Play-Making questions whether a theme in abstract form
ought to be the starting point of a play. Such a play
is "apt to advertise its origin." There are many such in
French literature but they "suffer artistically from the
obtrusive predominance of the theme—that is to say,
the abstract element—over the human and concrete
factors in the composition." The safer way would seem
to be to begin with a story, to devote all one's energies
to the invention of a thoroughly engrossing action, trust-
ing that one's ideas, if they have the compulsive power
of conviction, will find embodiment and utterance in

the characters and the dialogue without the playwright's having to attend to them directly.

Second Overture is one of Mr. Anderson's most successful embodiments of an important theme, the idea completely and excitingly dramatized. *The Feast of Ortolans,* on the other hand, is an idea, not embodied but merely personified, every detail so plainly tagged as to be more embarrassingly obvious in its intention than medieval allegory, without the medieval excuse of naïvete.

The action of *Second Overture* takes place in a Russian execution chamber, a cellar in the village of Tiumen, east of Moscow, in 1918. An apparently haphazard, but really carefully chosen assortment of human beings, refugees, are huddled together on one side of the room; and the guards, who will not answer questions, stand at the other side. Among the refugees is one Gregor, an exile, escaped from the Siberian mines, who had participated in the uprising of 1905. Knowing his own capture to be a mistake, he reassures the others.

Gregor. My friends, since you are guilty of nothing that would demand punishment, you distress yourselves unduly. I take it upon myself to promise you that there will be no injustice done. It must be that you have misunderstood our revolution.

Lvov. Your revolution? Are you one of them?

Gregor. In a way, yes. No doubt you remember the uprising of 1905. I was arrested and sentenced as one of the leaders. It may be that you and I were opponents at that time. You wear a uniform.

Lvov. I have conveniently forgotten my military record.

Gregor. No matter. I bear no grudge. But I assure you that what we fought for in 1905 we have now won.—We fought for free speech, for civil rights, for the abolition of arbitrary and tyrannical power, such as was exercised by the Czar, such as was carried out, perhaps, under your orders. But the safety from oppression which was never vouchsafed us under your regime you shall receive under ours.[1]

Gregor is even more confident when he learns who the commissar is. He and Charash had been friends in the earlier struggle. The prisoners have nothing to fear from Charash. When Charash appears Gregor explains that all these people have been taken prisoner by mistake. But Charash is unmoved. He will save Gregor, but not the others.

Gregor. What is their crime?

Charash. Their crime
Is what they are. Yes—what they mean in the world!

Gregor. And what was ours when we heard a sentence read
That sent you off to prison, me into exile,
Under the Czar? Our crime was what we were—
And what we meant to have was a government
Of equal justice! And now, by some strange chance,
You are the government, but our equal justice
Is far away as ever! It's murder
To kill men for opinions! It's the terror
And tyranny back again![2]

Charash remains firm. Yet he is not a monster. He is acting on principle. They must die because they are

aristocrats, and they are tainted. They must die that
the earth may be clean.

Gregor declines release for himself.

Better to lose
Than lose your faith.

The execution of the prisoners is turned over to a
drunken captain named Krassin, who has done so much
killing, and so much drinking to forget the killing, that
he is beginning to break under the strain. Gregor observes this when Krassin comes in, and takes advantage
of it.

At first he does not answer when his name is called.
Then he says Gregor is not there. He unnerves Krassin
by accusing him of being drunk, and then of being
crazy. Finally he tells him he is shooting ghosts. When
he has Krassin completely undone, he upsets the table
and stamps on the candles. The prisoners crash the
door, seize a truck which was idling outside, and get
away.

Charash, hearing the commotion, comes back. Krassin reports what has happened but says it is not too late
to pursue them. Charash says, let them go, he had a
friend among them.

But Gregor has not fled with the rest. If the revolution is dead, he will die too.

This is violent action; yet considering the situation
and the issues at stake, it does not seem excessive. Mr.
Anderson has contrived an action perfect for the revelation he wished to make; and only in two or three

instances has he marred it by using language too generalized, phrases out of a conference on civil rights instead of the language of a life-and-death struggle. For all the violence of the action, this is not melodrama. The opening scene is classic in its simplicity: the bare room, whitewashed walls and ceiling, with only the table and the candles, and the group of refugees on one side and the silent guard on the other. The development of the action is likewise simple and straightforward. Yet there is development; this is not just an incident. There is in the exposition a surprising amount of looking backward and forward and out in several directions, which, with astonishing economy, gives a sense of fullness and a reality to the persons involved in the struggle. There is enough preliminary action in the breakdown of the young man, in the children's finding their father's name on the wall, in the ravings of the bishop, in Plehve's description of the commissar, and finally in Gregor's promise, to build up real suspense. And there is the effort to avert the tragedy.

There is even a fully developed recognition scene, which is, in Mr. Anderson's view of dramatic tradition, "the essence of tragedy":

> ... a discovery by the hero of some element in his environment or in his own soul of which he has not been aware—or which he has not taken sufficiently into account. ... A play should lead up to and away from a central crisis, and this crisis should consist in a discovery by the leading character which has an indelible effect on his thought and emotion and completely alters his course of action.[3]

This is exactly the case with Gregor. He has been devoted to the revolution, believing its object to be a new order—a government of reason, justice, and humanity. But he discovers in the crisis at Tiumen that the revolution has been corrupted by its own violence, that it has become a greater tyranny than the one it opposed; and the discovery leads him to alter his course, to withdraw his support from the perpetrators of the violence and cast his lot with the victims.

The action of the drama is sensational, as escape from a death chamber must inevitably be. Yet it is not melodrama—the sensational for its own sake. In melodrama Gregor would have fled with the rest. It is the violence of a conflict in which moral issues are at stake. It is tragedy; for Gregor has seen the collapse of his dream, the failure of the cause to which he has given his life. His last act is one of atonement for the violence which he has helped to set in motion. The hero of serious drama, by Mr. Anderson's definition,

> must pass through an experience which opens his eyes to an error of his own. He must learn through suffering. In a tragedy he suffers death itself as a consequence of his fault or his attempt to correct it, but before he dies he has become a nobler person because of his recognition of his fault and the consequent alteration of his course of action.[4]

All this Mr. Anderson has achieved in *Second Overture*, but through an action so absorbing that the reader is entirely unaware of the presence of Prospero at work.

Not so with *The Feast of Ortolans*. It is not a drama, an action in which the reader, identifying himself with

the hero, makes important discoveries. There is no
hero at all, and the author has already made all the
discoveries.

The play opens on a static scene, which remains
static. On the eve of the French Revolution a group
of writers, artists, and other intellectuals, with a few
representatives of the aristocracy, including Lafayette
and Philippe of Orleans, are seated about the dinner
table at the chateau of the Duke de Pompignan, twenty
miles from Paris. Most of the action takes place off
stage and is merely reported on stage and commented
upon in classic fashion by the assembled company. The
only action on stage is the conversation of the guests,
who are awaiting, they suppose, the serving of the feast
of ortolans, a ritual of long standing in the family of
their host. They are, in fact, awaiting the approach of
their doom—which is rapidly building up outside this
enclosed scene.

There is appropriate significance in the feast of
ortolans as a symbol of the exploitation of the French
peasantry in the eighteenth century. Ortolans—native
to most European countries and celebrated for the delicate flavor of their flesh—are not hunted in a sports-
manlike fashion, but are caught in nets and fattened
in the dark.

The apparent intention of the play is the kind of
ironic effect produced by characters on a stage who,
unaware of their impending fate, carry on gaily and
frivolously in the presence of death, and now and then
utter appalling statements which the audience knows
—but they do not know—are true. The play fails to

produce such an effect because the characters are not
sufficiently ignorant of what is about to happen. They
are not the usual group of arrogant nobles, indifferent
to the sufferings of the poor and incapable of imagining
the reversal of fortune which is about to come upon
them. They are a group of intellectual liberals who
have had much to do with promoting the revolution.
This is the new element in the otherwise traditional
material which could have resulted in an original play;
but the author failed to develop its possibilities. Even
these intellectuals have their blind spot, their inno-
cence. They do not expect the revolution to be violent;
and if it should prove to be so, they are confident
that they, being its supporters, could not be its victims.
Mr. Anderson, by retaining too much of the traditional
material, has misdirected the attention of the audience.
From the situation, and from the emphasis on the aristocracy rather than the intellectuality of the host and
his guests, we are led to expect the kind of violent
action we have come to associate with stories of the
French Revolution. But *The Feast of Ortolans* is almost
entirely lacking in suspense. The prophecy of La Harpe,
which seems to be intended to provide the ominous
note, is totally ineffective because it is used for no
purpose except to forewarn of the immediate death of
the host; and the audience knows and cares too little
about the host to feel any anxiety over his fate. Besides,
it is just such an outcome as we expect from such a
situation. Had the prophecy been used to bring on the
levity which leads to the tragic error, it could have
given a lift to the action; but the company had already

m̶a̶ ̶l̶e̶ the fatal mistake of calling for the woodcutter to eat with them.

Calling for the woodcutter is the crisis of the play. From the effort of this unusual company of aristocrats to acknowledge their common humanity with the workers an absorbing action might have evolved. But the effect is dissipated in discussion. Our emotions are not engaged.

Obviously the interest and the meaning of the play are not to be found in the action. They must, therefore, be sought in the dialogue. But here, too, the play fails. The conversation of this group of intellectuals should be brilliantly witty as well as double-edged in its meaning; but it is neither. For wit we have the tricky makeshift of a stage direction, (*More laughter with an undertone of conversation*), followed by this rather painful effort at elegant trifling:

Duchess du Gramont. Gentlemen, gentlemen, not all together please. You drown each other with wit, and we poor women are left wondering what was said—

Condorcet. Forgive us, Madame la Duchesse, but for this once you were not supposed to hear—

The Duchess. Not to hear—and why?

Condorcet. To spare your cheeks, madame, lest those who blush easily should never blush again without art, and lest those who blush by technique, as say, by holding the breath, or by pressure on the jugular, should do themselves a mischief.

Mlle. de Sombreuil. But I've heard nothing really scandalous for years. I'm quite out of practice with my blushing![5]

And when the conversation takes a serious turn and is meant to be weighted with ironic implications, the ominous note is missing; there is no suggestion of impending disaster. Everything in such a piece depends on language—on a special use of language—and the language here fails. With the important exception of the controlling symbol of the feast of ortolans, the words have no overtones. They say what they mean and no more. And even in the controlling image the overtones are wrong; for this particular group of persons were not engaged in promoting their own interests by keeping the workers in the dark.

The fact that this is a group of intellectuals would seem to justify the attempt at classical treatment. But the play is not a classical play, a new interpretation of a familiar story. It is the old romantic materials—situation, characters, and meaning—merely poured into a classical mold.

The attempted new interpretation is implicit in the choice of the theoretical reformers in place of the tyrannical nobles for the *dramatis personae*. This choice seems to promise a representation of what happens when intellectuals carelessly throw out their speculations to be picked up by persons incapable of handling such volatile stuff. The play might have been a hieroglyph of the atomic scientists, for example, irresponsibly placing their bomb in the hands of people who lack the moral character to decline the use of it. The fact that the play was written before 1945 does not obviate such an interpretation, since I am speaking of the intention of the work, not the intention of the author.

The intention of the author is obvious; it has informed many of Mr. Anderson's plays. It is to illuminate contemporary issues by a dramatization of historical events. He had used the method with great success earlier, but here he has spoiled the effect by underscoring the parallels. The language is too modern: "The lower classes are badly paid"; "it's that confounded national deficit"; "we're promised a balanced budget"; the government's so easy with money." The reader would accept the ideas as coming from the eighteenth century if the language were a little less familiar; but the language suggests that the dialogue was created for the purpose of making a point rather than making a play. The peculiar weakness of Mr. Anderson's use of historical materials is that the audience is often made to suspect that he selected or invented his evidence to fit the conclusions he had in view. To be sure, all plays are contrived; but certainly the reader should not be made so acutely aware of the presence of the playmaker producing his effects.

The greatest possible contrast to Mr. Anderson's failure with historical materials in *The Feast of Ortolans* is presented by his magnificent achievement in *Elizabeth the Queen* and *Mary of Scotland*.

---

[1] Maxwell Anderson, *Second Overture,* in *Eleven Verse Plays,* Harcourt, Brace and Company, New York, 1940, p. 5.

[2] *Ibid.,* p. 14.

[3] ———, *Off Broadway,* William Sloane Associates, Inc., New York, 1947, p. 59.

[4] *Ibid.,* p. 61.

[5] ———, The *Feast of Ortolans,* in *Eleven Verse Plays,* pp. 3-4.

CHAPTER III

The Tudor Trilogy:
The Will to Power

I am indebted to John Gassner for the suggestion that
Anne of the Thousand Days, Mary of Scotland, and
Elizabeth the Queen (though written in reverse order)
may be regarded as a Tudor trilogy. They do actually
form a group, not only in their use of sixteenth-century
English history, but also in their unity of theme: the lust
for power in conflict with sexual passion. It is a great
theme; and in *Mary of Scotland* and *Elizabeth the Queen*
it is greatly dramatized. But *Anne of the Thousand Days*
is a weak play; and except for the unity of subject matter
and theme, it would scarcely occur to the reader to
compare it with the others. The form is not appropriate
to the subect matter or to the intended effect. "A play
of memory" cannot have the impact of immediacy required for the tragic effect. And the technique of styl-
ized action, a brilliant device for humorous or satiric
effect, is entirely unsuited to tragedy. It appeals too
exclusively to the intellect, too little to the emotions.

One feels no anxiety about Henry's guilt or Anne's fate as they appear in photographic pose in their separate spotlights, commenting reflectively upon their separate conditions. Even in the trial scene one is not held in the grip of contending passions. One follows with only the mildest interest the not very ingenious modulation of a Star Chamber action into a Communist fake trial. As a dramatic action it is as "fixed" as the kind of action it is intended to burlesque.

Mary of Scotland, on the other hand, has everything which a play needs for good theatre and good reading. It is entirely conventional—there is not a single new device in it—but the conventions are all used with consummate skill.

The opening scene is Shakespearean in design. The spectacle is arresting: a stormy night on a pier, "the tall piles of the background and the planks underfoot shine black and icy with their coating of freezing rain," the only light, the lantern of the two men playing cards "on the head of a fish-tub in the lee of a great coil of rope."

The entrance of the leading character is delayed, but anticipated by the remarks of those on stage. Necessary information is provided. The tone is set. It is an ominous tone: the wind, the sleet, the darkness, the indifference of the guard, the lack of preparation for receiving a person of importance, and the dour old Knox muttering his imprecations. And then, like a burst of sunlight, into this dismal scene come youth, and beauty and charm—the irresistible Stuart charm, which carries all before it.

How much of the whole play is prefigured in this opening scene! We watch with delight the queen's conquest of the surly old subject who has come to blast her good hopes and good intentions with such ugly phrases as "the whore of Babylon—the leprous and cankerous evangel of the Beast!" He believes he is forearmed by his knowledge of her character, and can risk the encounter. "I came myself to see this white face they speak of, and these taking graces." It was a mistake. He is no more immune to the taking graces than others. After her first words to him he is obliged to remind himself, "Aye, they told me you spoke honey—" He has tasted the honey now and knows its sweetness. He struggles valiantly. "Woman, I remember whose daughter and whose voice you are—" But he is no match for the winning appeal, "If I were your daughter, Master Knox . . . " He clings doggedly to his original intention, "I have said what I came to say." But his address, in their brief exchange, has progressed from "whore" to "woman" to "Madam" to "Your Majesty." And from spewing vile denunciations, he has been raised to the simple dignity of "I should be untrue to myself and my calling if I refused counsel where it is asked."

However much we may enjoy Mary's victory over Knox, her desire to win her subjects and rule well is not altogether the pure high-minded thing she thinks it, as Bothwell will tell her later. Her arsenal of Christian virtues does not contain self-sacrifice. And her worldly wisdom does not contain the capacity to look squarely at the realities with which she has to cope. She does not realize how much of what she imagines to be generosity, sincerity, and humility are only a kind of superb courtesy.

Elizabeth's first appearance is equally impressive, equally portentous, and a magnificent contrast. In her study at Whitehall she and Burghley take stock of their situation and lay their plans.

Burghley. I have set down the facts as we must face them, and alternative policies.

The facts are these: Mary Stuart has crossed from France to Scotland; she has been crowned; she is a Catholic, and related by blood to the most powerful house in France; she is an heir to the throne of England and considered by Catholics to be the rightful queen; Elizabeth is considered by Catholic Europe to be illegitimate.

There is nothing artificial about such exposition, nothing reminding the reader that it is contrived. A queen and her minister must face these facts and decide upon policies.

Burghley. . . . these things being true, Your Majesty must not allow Marie Stuart to succeed as Queen of Scotland. For in so far as she is secure in Scotland you are insecure in England.

Burghley's recommendation is war; but Elizabeth resists that proposal. War is difficult, costly, and hazardous. She sees another course.

Elizabeth. . . . you have overlooked in your summary two considerations which simplify the problem. One is the internal dissension in Scotland, half Protestant, half Catholic, and divided in a mortal enmity—

Burghley. Overlooked it! Madame, it is the main argument for an immediate declaration of war—Edinburgh would rally to your arms overnight! This is our opportunity to unite England and Scotland!

Elizabeth. A war would unite Scotland against us—unite Scotland under Mary. No—it is necessary first to undermine her with her own subjects.

Burghley. And how would that be accomplished?

Elizabeth. This brings me to the second consideration which you overlook—the conduct and reputation of Mary herself.

Burghley. Would that affect our policy?[1]

They have a letter from one of their agents reporting on Mary's conduct. Elizabeth observes that even the agent is apparently enamored. Then she resumes:

Elizabeth. My lord, my lord, it is hard to thrust a queen from her throne, but suppose a queen were led to destroy herself, led carefully from one step to another in a long descent until at last she stood condemned among her own subjects, barren of royalty, stripped of force, and the people of Scotland were to deal with her for us?[2]

Elizabeth is diabolical in her shrewd and ruthless calculations, worthy of comparison with the greatest of cold-blooded villains, Iago, and with something too of Richard III in her frank avowal of her own viciousness. When Burghley asks, "Can this be done?" she answers,

She is a woman, remember and open to attack as a woman. We shall set tongues wagging about her. And since it may be true that she is of a keen and noble mind, let us take care of that too. Let us marry her to a weakling and a fool. A woman's mind and spirit are no better than those of the man she lies under in the night.[3]

This is appalling. Is there motivation, is there even excuse for such malignity? That "she is next heir to my throne; she will hope for children to sit on it," can hardly account for such venom. A monarch must have a successor, and Elizabeth has nothing but loathing for the idea of providing one herself. "A queen who marries is no queen, a woman who marries is a puppet." If the successor were Mary's son, the object already mentioned of uniting England and Scotland would be accomplished. How can Elizabeth desire that her successor shall be the son of a weakling and a fool? Even the understandable anxiety over the immediate threat to her own person is an insufficient explanation of the violence of the language in which she describes the ruin she plans for Mary. Only jealousy can account for such deadly malice, the jealousy of a woman equal in power and prestige but inferior in personal attractiveness, the resentment of one deficient in ardor pretending scorn of the passion she cannot feel: "And she will marry—she must marry to staunch that Stuart blood."

Not that Elizabeth will have it thought that she is deficient in passion. "You would say that I am in myself more nearly what will be said of her." But neither her jealousy nor her amours cause her to forget for one moment the thing that really matters to her—her power, her throne. "But that is not what is said of me. Whatever I may be, it shall be said only that I am the queen of England, and that I rule well."

What the condition of the world might be if governments were under the management of women has fur-
nished matter for interesting speculations. Elizabeth was
guided in certain of her policies, particularly in financial
matters, by a feminine cautiousness and conservatism,
and in all her policies by a feminine preference for
subtlety rather than boldness. Mr. Anderson left her as
he found her in these respects, for history so far served
his purpose. He achieved a wonderfully dramatic balance by ascribing to the exquisitely feminine Mary the
same tenacious will to power and the same preference
for means other than war. And so the stage is set for a
deadly struggle.

The third scene of Act I is structurally out of place.
It ought to be in Act II; for while it is a counterpart to
Scene II in its presentation of Mary with her chief sup-
porter and of her defiance of Elizabeth, the decision
Mary makes is the crisis in her struggle and everything
that follows is consequence.

Mary's principal ally is her suitor, and his wooing is
forthright. But he does not prosper as a lover because
as a counsellor he is equally forthright. He warns Mary
of her danger, especially of the danger in herself. She
is becoming too circumspect.

She admits her love, but distrusts it.

Mary. . . . Our minds are not the same. If I gave my hand
To you, I should be pledged to rule by wrath
And violence, to take without denial,
And mount on others' ruin. That's your way
And it's not mine.

Bothwell. You'll find no better way.
There's no other way for this nation of churls and cravens.[4]

She does not believe it. When he pleads,

Take my help, take my hands!

She answers,

I would I could take both.
God knows how I wish it. But as I am queen
My heart shall not betray me, what I believe
And my faith. This is my faith, dear my lord, that all men
Love better good than evil, cling rather to truth
Than falseness, answer fair dealing with fair return;
And this too; those thrones will fall that are built on blood
And craft, that as you'd rule long, you must rule well—
This has been true, and is true

Bothwell can say only,

God help thee, child.[5]

When Elizabeth's emissary arrives Mary falls easily
into the trap they have set for her—too easily, considering
the warning she has had, and has again, before she acts,
from the man she knows to be her friend.

Bothwell. . . . Trust
Not one word they say to you, trust not even the anger
Their words rouse in you. They calculate effects.

But she does trust her anger and her resentment.

Mary. For, hear me, my lord of Bothwell.
I too have a will—a will as strong as your own,
And enemies of my own, and my long revenges
To carry through. I will have my way in my time
Though it burn my heart out and yours.

And after his reply to this, she says,

Look, Bothwell. I am a sovereign,
And you obey no one. Were I married to you I'd be
Your woman to sleep with. You'd be king here in Edinburgh,
And I'd have no mind to your ruling.[6]

This is the confession of her tragic weakness: she will
not share or delegate or relinquish her power. Further-
more, they have attacked her Stuart blood, and she is
jealous of that blood. They have made her angry. "They'll
meet more anger than they know."

Once more he warns her. And once more he offers
his love and his support. But now she denies even her
love.

Mary. Oh, what's a little love, a trick of the eyes,
A liking, to be set beside the name
You'll have forever, or your son will have?

Bothwell. Well, it's been nibbling at you this long while,
And now it's got you, the blight of Charlemagne—
The itch to conquer.[7]

Act II is the dreary spectacle of Elizabeth's calculated
effects working out exactly as calculated. Another friend
and advisor counsels Mary, as Bothwell had, to take a
firm hand. But though she insists on playing the game of

power and pride and little revenges, she spurns the weapons of that game. Bothwell risks all to save her; but she had destroyed all when she decided to rely on faith and tolerance and forbearance and fair dealing to gain the ends required by power and pride.

The last act is highly effective dramatically, with the two women facing one another, with the irony of Mary's appeal, as woman to woman, when it was through her womanhood that Elizabeth ruined her, and with Mary's final triumph, again as a woman.

There is no preachment here, though there is meaning for our time and for all time. The thirst for power, the struggle for power, and what that struggle involves: this play explores the issues, but it draws no conclusions. The reader must draw his own conclusions.

Even the prophecies are effective here, for the ironies remain. "Those thrones will fall that are built on blood and craft," Mary says; and we feel it must be so. Yet the throne of England stood, and not only stood but absorbed the throne of Scotland. And whatever we discover of Elizabeth's craft and perfidy and cruelty, we go on saying she ruled well. And Mary, though she could not rule, supplied the throne of England with the line of rulers who succeeded Elizabeth.

That Elizabeth is an able ruler is the whole meaning of her tragedy. What Maxwell Anderson had to say in *Elizabeth the Queen* (1930) to a world once more falling under the spell of personal rule was that the ability to rule is not a divine right but a tragic flaw.

The situation in the two plays is the same: the lust for power in conflict with love, the queen unable to

share her throne because she knows her lover will take
over, will become king, and unable to believe altogether
in his love for herself, knowing the lure of power. But
here it is the queen who is cool and firm and farseeing.
Elizabeth tries to protect Essex by warning him against
himself as well as against the other ministers who are
seeking to destroy him. But his pride and his temper are
not to be curbed by policy.

"Can a man quarrel on order or avoid a quarrel at
will?" he exclaims impatiently.

"Why certainly," Bacon answers, "if he knows his
way."

"Not I," Essex retorts.

So far Essex is like Mary. He falls easily into the trap
which is set for him. But Essex and Bothwell are also
much alike, though Bothwell is the more generous lover.
Both men believe that governments require the boldness
and firmness of a man at their head; but Bothwell, in the
end, will yield all to save the queen, though to save her
as queen is to lose her for himself.

In *Elizabeth the Queen* the question of whether the
man or the woman is the better ruler is central to the
conflict. And nowhere is Mr. Anderson more successful
in character delineation and in allowing character to
determine the action and the outcome of the action.
I cannot agree with Barrett H. Clark that the action is
contrived, except in the sense that all plays are contrived.[8] Are we expected to believe when we read the
first line of *Antony and Cleopatra*, "Nay, but this dotage
of our General o'erflows the measure," that Shakespeare

does not have the end of the play in view? It is what Elizabeth and Essex are that determines the course of the action; and what they are is something quite believable.

Elizabeth is no mere feminist, asserting woman's equality with man. She is as confident of her superiority as Essex is of his. "You believe you'd rule England better/Because you're a man!" she says to Essex.

Essex. That last is true. I would.
And that doesn't mean I don't love you ... remember that.
I love you, my queen, madly, beyond all measure,
But that's not to say I cannot see where you fail
As sovereign here, and see that why you fail
When you do is merely because a woman cannot
Act and think like a man.

Elizabeth. Act and think like a man ... !
Why should I
Think like a man when a woman's thinking's wiser?[9]

To follow her thinking and acting as she threads her way through the mesh of intrigues which surround her is as fascinating a pursuit as literature has to offer. Her skill in handling complex situations amounts to genius. Essex thinks it amounts to cowardice, and tells her so plainly on several occasions. It is the chief cause of contention between them.

Yet she is no coward. It is his masculine notion that it is more courageous to blaze forth armed to the teeth, to strike first where you know you have the advantage of arms and position and skill, than to stand unarmed in the midst of peril, refusing to provoke or to aggravate the danger by showing fear or anger. When word is brought of the rebellion of Essex, Elizabeth instructs her officer,

Whatever orders
You receive from your superiors, whatever broils
Occur, he is to have free access to my presence.

Armin. There would be danger to your person, madame.

Elizabeth. I will risk that.[10]

And she does risk it, even to the point of permitting Essex to take possession of the palace. Her strategy is brilliant in its recognition of the human weaknesses on which it depends for its success. She has no fear of the London rabble, because she knows they have no real grievances. Her reign has given them peace and prosperity. There is in them no fury of oppression suddenly thrown off. They are merely excited by a popular military leader.

"What is the Lord Mayor doing about this?" she asks the herald.

"Nothing, madame," he answers.

"How like a lord mayor and how sensible," she says. "That's the first principle of government. Never do anything. Let the others make all the mistakes."

Even her little joke with the players is sound political wisdom. She knows the value of humor in a tense situation. There is humor, but there is more than humor too in her every move.

Elizabeth. . . . Is my kingdom so shaky that we dare not listen to a true history? Are my people so easily led that the sight of a king deposed in play will send them running thither to pull the queen out of her chair? Have we not passion plays in ever little town showing the murder of our Lord? You are nervous, Lord Burghley. Let these children play their plays.

Cecil. Your Majesty, I very much fear they are not all children, and that they mean to do harm.

Elizabeth. Then let them. Let them do all the harm they can. Are we too stupid to see that to prohibit a rebellious play is to proclaim our fear of rebellion? Who is there here who fears a rebellion against me? I do not.

Cecil. It is dangerous to let these mutterings grow, dear queen.

Elizabeth. It is dangerous to touch them. Let them mutter, if they will. Let them cry out . . . let them run the streets, these children! When they have worn themselves weary running and crying "Up with Essex!" "Down with Elizabeth!" and got themselves drunk in mutual pledges, they will go to bed and sleep soundly and wake up wiser.[11]

Of course the most impressive exhibition of her genius for governing is her recovery of the palace after she has deliberately allowed Essex to take it. But this scene we cannot watch with detachment, with admiration for and delight in the brilliance of the moves and countermoves; for here too much is at stake. This is sheer tragedy, awful in its revelation that the very thing which is Elizabeth's greatness as a ruler is the thing which destroys her personal happiness. This is the crisis not only in the struggle between Elizabeth and Essex for supreme power, but also in the conflict between power and love.

Mr. Anderson has given us only brief glimpses of Elizabeth as a woman in love; but they are sufficient to indicate that her love is no giddy reversion to youth, but the love of a mature woman, full of the understanding of life. Haunted always by doubts because of the disparity of their ages, she begs her lover to tell her when he shall have tired of her, to tell her first before others see it and laugh at her. "Will you do that, in all kindness, in memory of great love past?" But then she adds, "No. You could not, could not. It's not in a man to be kind that way, nor in a woman to take it kindly."

No more convincing evidence of her real attractiveness could have been imagined than the generosity she inspires in her young rival, Penelope.

Elizabeth. Do you love him well, my dear?

Penelope. Yes, Your Majesty.

(ELIZABETH *bows her head wearily on* PENELOPE)

Elizabeth. I love him. He has never loved me.

Penelope. Yes, yes. He does love you. I've been madly jealous of you.

Elizabeth. Of me? Poor child.

Penelope. But he loved you . . . and never me at all.

Elizabeth. How do you know?

Penelope. He told me.

Elizabeth. What did he say?

Penelope. He said, "I love her dearly." I wanted him for myself, and I warned him against you. He laughed at me. He said, "I love her very dearly."

Elizabeth. You tell me this because you want to save him.

Penelope. No, dear queen. It's true.[12]

She asks Penelope not to be present when Essex comes for the last time.

Elizabeth. . . . Dear, you're so young. Do not be here when he
    comes. . . .
Do you mind? You'll look so young.

Penelope. Yes, madam . . . but you . . .
You're beautiful.[13]

The tragic flaw in both Mary and Essex is that they waver between power and love, destroying their love by their cunning and losing the power game through love. The candor and trustfulness which love requires are inimical to the power game. Elizabeth does not waver. At the moment of Elizabeth's surrender—or is it only the last subtle maneuver to safeguard her power?—she says,

Love, I will be
Your servant. Command me. What would you have?

Essex is compelled by the sincerity which love inspires to confess:

I am troubled to be dishonest. I have brought my army
Here to the palace—and though it's all true what we've said—
No letters—utter agony over long months—
It is something in myself that has made me do this,
Not Cecil—not anyone. No one but myself.
The rest is all excuse.[14]

She leads him on to confess the extent of his ambition;
and finally by acknowledging—or pretending to acknowledge—herself his prisoner, she disarms him completely.
Believing himself victorious, he thinks he can afford to
be generous, to grant her her freedom. He does not know
what power requires. But she knows, and she does not
flinch. He trusts her word, and she betrays his trust.
When he gives the order to return the palace to her as
proof of his love and trust, he says, "This is our last
quarrel," and she answers with terrible irony, "Yes, our
last." She has chosen power knowing its price. "I have
ruled England a long time, my Essex, and I have found
that he who would rule must be quite friendless, without
mercy, without love."

This is great tragedy in the traditional sense, not to
be disparaged for its traditional character, as Joseph
Wood Krutch does so disparage it.

> *Elizabeth the Queen* was hailed as something new in our
> theater because it was a romantic tragedy in verse, but
> except upon the surface its novelty is far from absolute.
> There is little in it more unexpected to us than it would
> have been to our grandfathers, and this is true whether one
> thinks of the form or the substance. Mr. Anderson did not
> invent a tragedy or a tragic view of any series of events;
> he revived one. . . . And what is true of *Elizabeth the Queen*

is equally true of *Mary of Scotland* and *Valley Forge*. However agreeable any one them may be as a stage spectacle, none actually creates a new tragic pattern or reveals in the story it tells a tragic meaning hitherto unperceived.[15]

Assuming that genius must always be original, Krutch failed to see that the very lack of originality in *Elizabeth the Queen* was vital to the revelation which it made. For it is not true that the story it tells reveals no new meaning. It is because the meaning is (or was, in 1930) so very new that the familiar story and traditional form were important. Mr. Anderson's judgment in putting his new wine into an old bottle was aesthetically sound. He thereby secured for his new interpretation of power the full impact of its newness. For a convincing demonstration that power—not just the abuse of power, but power itself—is evil, and that it is disastrous, not only to those over whom it is exercised, but even to those possessing it, no form could be more appropriate than a revival of "the grand romantic manner," in which power had hitherto been glorified.

It is true that the manner itself was greeted with enthusiasm; but again Krutch misunderstood the fact which he observed. We hailed romantic tragedy in verse, not "as something new in our theater," but as something old which still had validity. To Americans in the early thirties, whose self-confidence and self-respect had suffered the successive shocks of muckraking, behavioristic psychology, the First World War, the debunking spirit of the twenties, and finally the collapse of our boasted economic system, whose mood was best expressed by

God in *The Green Pastures,* "Everything dat's fastened down is comin' loose," Maxwell Anderson's embodiment of contemporary attitudes in the well-known, well-loved form of the past was reassurance not to be despised. To find even our humor, our slang and nonsense, wearing the Elizabethan dress, and looking quite at ease in it, was good fun. To find our modern distrust of power a heroic concept capable of wearing the purple was a spiritual boon, far more valuable than any mere novelty of form could possibly have provided.

1 Maxwell Anderson, *Mary of Scotland,* in *Eleven Verse Plays,* Harcourt Brace and Company, New York, 1940, Act I, Scene II, pp. 17-19.

2 *Ibid.,* p. 21.

3 *Ibid.,* p. 21.

4 *Ibid.,* Act I, Scene III, p. 36.

5 *Ibid.,* p. 37.

6 *Ibid.,* pp. 57-59.

7 *Ibid.,* p. 61.

8 Barrett H. Clark, *Maxwell Anderson, the Man and His Plays,* Samuel French, New York, 1933, p. 24.

9 Maxwell Anderson, *Elizabeth the Queen,* in *Eleven Verse Plays,* Act I, Scene II, pp. 30-31.

10 *Ibid.,* Act II, Scene I, p. 69.

11 *Ibid.,* Act II, Scene III, p. 84.

12 *Ibid.,* Act III, p. 113.

13 *Ibid.,* p. 122.

14 *Ibid.,* Act II, Scene III, pp. 99-100.

15 Joseph Wood Krutch, *The American Drama Since 1918,* Random House, New York, 1939, pp. 291-292.

CHAPTER IV

The Quest
for Freedom

It is a natural transition from Maxwell Anderson's dramatic treatment of the theme of personal power to his exploration of that kind of government with which the so-called "free world" is opposing the resurgence of dictatorship. Exploration is the only possible word to use in this connection, and it calls to mind Mark Schorer's essay "Technique as Discovery." Schorer developed his strategy for dealing with fiction, but I think we shall find it a valuable aid to the discussion we now have in hand.

I have already mentioned in another connection Mr. Anderson's suspicion of those large affirmations by which many writers in the past robbed faith of its essential character of commitment to "things hoped for" rather than things certain. Even though he regards the playwright as prophet, he, as playwright, has no resounding convictions to proclaim. He is a humble seeker of the truth; and nowhere is he more tentative in his statements

than in his quest for the meaning of freedom. He has no
great insights to communicate; he has only a few spiritual
hypotheses which he is subjecting to the test of artistic
formulation.

For his exploration of the eternal conflict between
freedom and government we must consider together five
plays so diverse in form that the grouping would by any
traditional view of drama seem absurd. Yet their very
diversity is of the greatest importance; for Mr. Anderson
does actually submit his content to the test of form for
the purpose of discovering its meaning and its value.

Early in the thirties Americans—even the least
thoughtful among us——were compelled by our own economic and political failures, as well as by the challenges
of totalitarianism, to re-examine "those truths" which we
had supposed were "self-evident." Such times—times of
uncertainty for a whole people—are generally acknowledged to be unlucky for the creative artist. As Matthew
Arnold explained the matter nearly a hundred years ago,
it is not the function of the creative artist to discover new
ideas. That is the business of the philosopher. The creative artist appropriates as the elements of his art the
best ideas current in his own time and, by a process of
synthesis and exposition, turns them into objects of
beauty—that is, works of art.

T. S. Eliot reiterates the doctrine that it is not the
business of the creative artist to be an original thinker,
but he does not regard the fact as inimical to the production of great works of art. Shakespeare is no less a
poet than Dante even though the system of thought

behind Shakespeare was not so great as that behind
Dante.

> The great poet, in writing himself, writes his time.... If
> Shakespeare had written according to a better philosophy,
> he would have written worse poetry; it was his business to
> express the greatest emotional intensity of his time, based
> on whatever his time happened to think.[1]

Maxwell Anderson agrees with Mr. Eliot that the
artist cannot transcend the thought of his time, but his
attitude toward the fact harks back to Matthew Arnold.
He regards it as a misfortune to be born into a time
when the thinking is trivial or confused. "Every artist is
at a loss in a confused civilization, but the playwright
is in the worst plight of all." For, as Mr. Anderson sees
it, the audience demands that a play shall have meaning
and that the playwright shall represent that meaning in
terms of his own generation. "There is no instance in
the theatre of a writer who left behind him a body of
unappreciated work which slowly found its public, as,
for example, the work of Shelley and Keats found a
belated public after they had left the scene."

Poets and fiction writers might express the cynicism
or despair of certain minorities; but the mood of the
majority of Americans in the early thirties was less extreme. There was a critical spirit which responded to
social and political satire; and there was an effort to
recover the values which had, presumably, produced the
democratic way of life, and might be expected to restore
it if they could be revived. Novelists and playwrights

turned to our own national past for subjects. And even
historians abandoned the pose of critical impartiality
and wrote histories with such an avowed bias as that
revealed by the title *Epic of America*. Maxwell Anderson
capitalized on both these moods.

His first contribution to the movement was a political
satire entitled *Both Your Houses*, first produced in 1933.
It is an important play, not only for being the first of
its kind, but also for being good in its kind. There is
little good political satire in American drama. Our playwrights have very generally been heavy-handed in their
attempts at satire. Mr. Anderson possessed a spirit of
genuine playfulness, an indispensable resource for a
playwright, which shows itself more clearly in later plays,
but which undoubtedly operated to preserve this play
from preachment. The comment of John Mason Brown,
written at the time, is of interest not only for its revelation of the receptivity of the public to such sharp criticism of the American system, but also for Mr. Brown's
recognition on the spot of the intrinsic merits of the play.

> By having kept his temper in the writing of *Both Your
> Houses*, Maxwell Anderson has got the better not only of
> his subject and his audience but also of his fellow-drama-
> tists who of recent years have attempted to turn the stage
> into a forum for the discussion of public questions. With
> the calm detachment usually reserved for the penning of
> drawing-room comedies, he has held up to the patrons of
> the Theatre Guild as merciless and disheartening a picture
> of governmental corruption as anyone could imagine. It is
> a shocking, bitter indictment, calculated to raise doubts in
> the hearts of even the staunchest supporters of the demo-
> cratic ideal.[2]

One is under the strongest temptation to quote some
of the speeches in which that indictment is most brilliantly expressed, for they are the neatest little packets
of political cynicism to be found anywhere in American
drama. Yet to detach them from their context is to de-
prive them of their greatest merit; for whatever independent validity they may have, they are entirely dramatic, and the reader or playgoer should not be cheated
of the greater impact they have in context.

The substance of the indictment is that honest government is rare in any form but impossible in a democracy,
that graft is the principal business of government and
order only a by-product necessary to the grafters, that
political gangsterism created prosperity and if allowed
to resume its operations will revive it, that the voters
are utterly stupid and incompetent and as self-centered
and grasping in their small way as the politicians are in
their big way. Yet as Mr. Brown points out, these un-
scrupulous politicians are no monsters.

> His play has no villains in it in the melodramatic sense of
> the word. His lawmakers may legislate as if they were so
> many public enemies, but personally they are agreeable
> and ingratiating people. They are the victims of a system;
> hardened politicians who believe in expediency and are
> accustomed to bargaining for votes. They know the game
> as Mr. Anderson's novice from Nevada does not, and they
> play it for all that it is worth. Yet they are pleasant enough
> men and the most crafty and unscrupulous among them is
> the most winning character in the play.[3]

There is likewise no hero in the melodramatic sense.
The novice from Nevada, Alan McClean, got himself

elected to Congress as a result of having been fired from a teaching job for exposing the misappropriation of endowment funds. He is pledged to work for the completion of a Nevada dam, and has been put on the House Appropriations Committee. But the first thing he does in Washington is to have his own election investigated. Thereupon, he discovers that his backer and campaign manager had an understanding with the contractors and that the forty million dollars being appropriated for the dam is more than would be required had the bidding been honest. He further discovers that several members of the Appropriations Committee stand to gain personally by the more than two hundred million dollars worth of additional projects included in the bill for the dam, ostensibly for the purpose of securing the necessary votes. He breaks up the first committee meeting he attends by asking innocently a lot of embarrassing questions, and by declaring that he is no longer for the bill.

Maxwell Anderson does not achieve his exposé of the failures of "the people," as Ibsen does in his *Enemy of the People,* through self-righteous tirades on the part of the hero and an action from which he emerges morally unscathed. John Mason Brown attributes Mr. Anderson's success with political satire to his refusal to see red. I should say it is far more the result of his refusal to see black and white. McClean gets his initiation into practical politics through an action so complex in its tangle of conflicting interests and cross-purposes that he comes out of it asking in sheer bewilderment and very humbly, "Is honesty possible here at all?"

Yet for all its serious implications, the play is highly

entertaining, not only in the cynical dialogue, but even in the central action in which the hero defeats his own ends by trying to beat his adversaries at their own game of clever manipulation. Finding himself balked in his efforts to purge the bill of graft, McClean puts back into it everything which anyone has asked for, hoping to defeat it by making it a monstrosity. But everyone is delighted, the bill is passed, and McClean, to his chagrin, is acclaimed a political genius.

In the general rejoicing which follows the passage of the bill one of the committee members say, ironically, "There's never been a better government on the face of the earth! Our forefathers fought and died to give us the government we have today!" Mr. Anderson's denial of that patriotic cant is the subject of the next play.

Valley Forge is not a good play. Or rather, it is not so good a play as it could have been. The first two acts are an unpromising preparation for a very good third act. And, as is often the case when Mr. Anderson is disappointing, the failures appear to be such as might very easily have been avoided. There was no need, for instance, to try to alter our preconceived idea of George Washington. Nothing in the plot requires it. And there are limits to the freedom which a creative artist may exercise in handling historical figures. The only reasons for employing historical materials in imaginative writing are for the richness of association they bring to the work, and for enlarging insights already possessed by the reader. To alter the material beyond recognition is, then, to destroy its value. It is true that George Washington is generally regarded as an unsuitable character for fictional or dramatic treatment, because he is felt to be not altogether "human." Yet for this particular play the Washington of tradition—dignified, reserved, somewhat formal in speech and manner, idealistic, courageous, stern with himself but tenderly concerned for his men in their suffering—this Washington, with only a shift of emphasis from the more heroic qualities to the tender regard for his troops and the discouragement which must have been his in the face of his betrayal by Congress, is all that the play requires. It is the author who required something else.

Mr. Anderson tried to express in this play some of the ideas about government and about freedom which are his own convictions, and which he has stated with admirable clarity and force in his preface to *Knickerbocker Holiday*. And he might have succeeded, for he has contrived an action which demands discussion of the issues and principles involved in the Revolution. But the dialogue is not right. The speeches have too much the character of something said for its own sake or for its effect on a twentieth-century audience. The speakers see too far and too clearly for men who are finding their way as they go, struggling to bring into being "something that's never been on this earth,... something that's never existed." They know all about this something that has never existed. Lucifer Tench, a mere professional soldier, speaks as cynically of the new government in prospect as Sol Fitzmaurice, in *Both Your Houses*, speaks out of a long personal and national retrospect. And the speeches of Washington are even more incredible for not being such as we expect from the man we think we know.

Aristocrat that he was, it is not at all incredible that he
should say, "Men are mostly fools" and "They'll govern
themselves like fools." But aristocrat that he was, he
never would have said such a thing to the fools themselves, especially when they were the starving, ragged
men of his army.

Of course it is the aristocratic taint which Mr.
Anderson wishes to eliminate. He has a concept of the
type of character which produces and is produced by
freedom: simple, stubborn, men of earth; slow-thinking,
but sound of instinct; suspicious of any profession of
high principles; preserved from great crimes solely by
the lack of opportunity in the "blessed inefficiency" of
democracy; and arriving at the ultimate wisdom of life
by sheer blunder. He has tried several times to give this
idea dramatic embodiment, and such characters are
convincing enough when they are all fiction. But the
effect of drawing men like Washington and Socrates
with such lineaments is ludicrous.

Great men are quite likely to be humble men, and to
speak and act simply. But Mr. Anderson never seems to
be quite sure he has humility and simplicity unless he
adds a touch of vulgarity, and sometimes even a little
stupidity. I doubt that any reader finds Mr. Anderson's
Washington more real for a sprinkling of "by Gods" in
his conversation, and a little plain talk about "sow-belly";
or believes that he ever would have seized a man by the
collar and the seat of his pants and thrown him out of
a meeting.

I do not regard, as do some other writers, the Mary
Philipse interlude as part of the effort to humanize

Washington. She is necessary to the plot. Only a woman
with a romantic interest in Washington, and touched by
what she had seen of the courage and suffering in
Washington's camp, would be so impulsive as to reveal
at the crucial moment the information that the French
had signed the assistance pact.

Maxwell Anderson is richly ingenious in the matter
of contriving dramatic situations and an absorbing action. He has the storyteller's gift and spends it gener-
ously. But in certain matters of style, particularly of
tone, he is sometimes unsure. That is his failure in
Valley Forge. He had a conflict of purposes which he
failed to resolve. He wished to say something positive
about freedom and the effects of freedom, and affirmations of that kind call for a certain lift in language and
cadence approaching if not actually attaining poetry.
And here he had both the personalities and the occasion
for such utterance. The reader is prepared to accept
from contemporaries of Thomas Jefferson and Edmund
Burke almost any degree of eloquence. But Washington
stands fumbling his words, as shy of an affirmation as
the chastened idealists of the twentieth century.

This is no lucky war for me. I thought it was at first. I wanted
to astound the world as a military leader, but my head's grayer
now and I've had enough of that. What I fight for now is a
dream, a mirage, perhaps, something that's never been on this
earth since men first worked it with their hands, something
that's never existed and will never exist unless we can make it
and put it here—the right of free-born men to govern themselves in their own way.—Now men are mostly fools, as you're
well aware. They'll govern themselves like fools. There are prob-

ably more fools to the square inch in the Continental Congress than in the Continental army, and the percentage runs high in both. But we've set our teeth and trained our guns against the hereditary right of arbitrary kings, and if we win it's curfew for all the kings of the world.—It may take a long time, but one by one, bolster themselves as they will, pour out money as they may for mercenaries, make what victorious wars they can, they'll slip one by one from their thrones and go out with the great wash through this breach we make in their sea walls.—It may not be worth the doing. When you deal with a king you deal with one fool, knave, madman, or whatever he may be. When you deal with a congress you deal with a conglomerate of fools, knaves, madmen and honest legislators, all pulling different directions and shouting each other down. So far the knaves and fools seem to have it. That's why we're stranded here on this barren side-hill, leaving a bloody trail in the snow and chewing the rotten remains of sow-belly on which some merchant has made his seven profits.—So far our government's as rotten as the sow-belly it sends us. I hope and pray it will get better. But whether it gets better or worse it's your own, by God, and you can do what you please with it—and what I fight for is your right to do what you please with your government and with yourselves without benefit of kings.—[4]

Even the young Lafayette is not permitted to give vent to his enthusiasm for the Revolution without much hesitation and apologizing for his "unfortunate eloquence."

There are three cross-purposes which thwart the poetic impulse in the early part of the play. The first is the distrust of all government, which had received adequate treatment in *Both Your Houses,* and is reiterated here because the author wished to point out that the founding fathers did not fight and die to give us good

government, but to give us the greatest possible freedom
from government. The second is that image of the free
man which I have already discussed, the man in whom
a kind of halting speech is taken to be the stamp of sincerity. The third is the most serious obstacle. It is the
realistic treatment of the hardships of the Continental
Army at Valley Forge. The truth of that matter is so far
stranger than fiction that it would wither the hardiest
poetic bloom. In fact, we can scarcely be expected to
take such stuff as entertainment even in prose. It is too
painful. The effect is not one of exaltation in the triumph
over terrible odds. The odds are not terrible; they are
disgusting.

But the play rises to its true tone at the end of Act II,
when Washington says to Mary,

Aye, once
I was alive, before so many men
had died around me.

There greatness speaks with genuine simplicity, not in
that self-conscious stammer which Mr. Anderson mistakes for the note of sincerity. And throughout the last
act the great man is allowed his greatness.

Washington cannot doff his power, that power which
resides not in what a man does but in what he is. Men
will follow such a man, because he is in very truth
"the way," the visible, tangible presence of what a man
may be. The only thing a leader can give his followers is
faith in themselves. Washington had said earlier, "This
is your fight more than mine"; but the moment he discovers they have accepted their responsibility, then it

becomes again his fight too. "I am servant to these men in the rags of homespun," he says to General Howe. "They've heard from me this proposition of the king's, and they refuse it flatly. This war, to your brief misfortune, is not mine to end but theirs." Here speaks the true democratic leader, not a benefactor doing something for men, but the organizer and director of men doing something for themselves. The tragic role of the benefactor, the benevolent dictator, concerns us next.

Whereas *Valley Forge* is a play of somewhat dubious value redeemed by its third act, the *Masque of Kings* is a great play only if the third act is lopped off. The comment which it adds is superfluous, for the issues and the meaning are perfectly dramatized in the first two acts; and the reappearance and suicide of Mary Vetsera, in the third act, distorts the play—spoils its symmetry— by giving to the love interest an importance which it does not actually have in the meaning of the drama.

Because of the power motif, as well as the form and tone of the play—a historical drama in verse—one is prompted to compare the *Masque of Kings* with the plays of the Tudor group. But the central conflict of the play is not between power and love, except as the love story is a symbol; the conflict is between power and freedom. Rudolph sees and states the issue clearly.

Rudolph. . . . I'm no jingling poet, to sell a crown
for love and a pair of shoes. If I wanted empire,
I'd have the empire, and you, and Stephanie,
and anything I whistled for! But when
I say the Habsburg crown's an ancestral curse
and I won't wear it, then the bars go up

around me, and I feel my father's hand
closing on what I do and where I go,
till the Hofburg's a prison, the street's a prison
where I ride, with yielding walls, but iron
and not to be broken through. Crown Prince I am,
Crown Prince I must be. This is my answer to them:
either I take the road free as a beggar,
or from now on my life's my own.[5]

So much for love. It is a symbol of freedom. But for
the freedom it symbolizes, for personal liberty—his right
to do as he pleases—Rudolph will not sell his crown. He
will use his power for beneficent purposes, to gain freedom for others as well as for himself, or he will renounce
it altogether as a thing inherently evil.

Rudolph. I'm not
an Alexander. What he stood for slipped
down the black hills in a very bloody sunset
when the first Napoleon died. There are two reasons
why I might wish to rule in Hungary;
let us look at them calmly. First, if the empire
drifts as it's drifting now, it will smash up
and I'll be left nothing to rule. Second, if I
were king I might inaugurate reforms
which I've worked all my life for, and which might
be in time to stave off ruin. Well, they're both
fallacious, both these reasons. If I seize
on Hungary, there'll be a war, and all reform
wiped out for a decade, what advance we've planned
toward tolerant government will be ridden down
not only in Austria, but by my orders
in Hungary, and the empire will break up
for the same sweet reasons we have now—dragoons
on every peasant's back—the forms of law

with absolutism behind them. Add to that
that I, on whom you pin your hopes of freedom,
would go the way of all the Habsburgs, lose
my liberal principles one by one, be driven
to give them up to hold a realm together,
and once committed to the adventure, doomed
to be my father over again, I'd catch
at desperate expedients, fill the gaps
in the falling walls with more and more lives of men;
acts of oppression, made to stiffen the line,
would harden into policies, we'd mix
our mortar out of the shambles of the dead
to build new bastions where more men might die
defending me, and my throne! If you're a soldier
you should know this.

John. Have you read in history
of any age when men have not been forced
to fight for freedom?

Sceps. There are times, Your Highness,
when the means are rendered gracious by the end,
though the means be evil. No war lasts forever,
nor would you change so much.

Rudolph. And that's fallacy!
A government will end as it begins,
and if it builds on slaughter it will stand
on slaughter till it falls![6]

Though Rudolph sees so clearly the nature of the
whole tendency of violent revolution, he is nevertheless
impelled irresistibly to it by the complex interplay of
forces in and around him: by the hopes his liberal views
have aroused in his friends, by his craving for personal

freedom, by the tensions in him produced by his own
unused abilities, by his father's firm resistance to all that
he desires, and finally by the explosive situation which
has developed in Hungary. Once more we must admire
Mr. Anderson's ingenuity in devising an absorbing action
out of the cross-purposes of men and women of diverse
character. In the heat of passion Rudolph rushes into an
adventure which his reason has condemned; and once
in it he strives to rationalize the deed and bring good out
of what he knows to be evil. In the unfolding of the
action and in his comments upon it we hear again Mr.
Anderson's comment upon contemporary events, though
in this play as in *Elizabeth the Queen* and *Mary of
Scotland,* but not in *The Feast of Ortolans,* the tone is
true to the historical subject matter, and the reader is
left to make his own application.

Rudolph. It was Napoleon Bonaparte, the runt,
who first worked out the formula still used
for consolidating conquest. Caesar, before him,
cut him a crop of kings, and then went on,
more or less bored to discover that new kings
sprang up behind him. But the young scrub Napoleon,
with a heart like that of a cheap Swiss watch, and the brain
of a coffin salesman, set out to sell his wares
by getting one foot indoors, and then proclaiming
his stuff was free, guaranteed, and a hundred years
to pay. He tried it first in Italy,
offering liberty, also fraternity,
equality gratis, and all they had to do
was let him buckle their shoulders into a collar
and the world was theirs. Our aim is not the same,
but the formula's still good. Our first six words

in Hungary tomorrow must be these:
We come to set you free.[7]

There is no mistaking the implication of these lines.
"We come to set you free" has been the promise of all
the modern dictators. And of the millions yearning for
freedom few have paused to ask whether the thing is
possible—whether one man by an exercise of authority,
or by yielding the control, can confer freedom on other
men. If they have questioned at all, it has been only the
intentions of the dictator, not his ability. And who can
know the secret intention?

Only the dramatist or storyteller. Sure of Rudolph's
motives, because he has created them, Mr. Anderson
can work out to its logical conclusion the tragic error
of the benevolent despot. What Alexander and Napoleon
stood for, what the Tudor rulers as Mr. Anderson represents them stood for—power for its own sake, the glory
of it, the magnificent distinction of possessing and ex-
ercising power—Rudolph utterly repudiates. Yet he desires power, for modern reasons—that he may use it for
the good of mankind. It is the reason put forth by all
the dictators. It is likewise the claim by which the defenders of freedom justify their meeting force with force
and violence with violence. Again Mr. Anderson has
presented the terrible ironies of the human dilemma,
and has not resolved them by any of the tricks of logic
or romance, but has let them take their tragic course.

Just at the moment when the hopes inspired by his
views have brought matters to a crisis in Hungary,
Rudolph is stung to wrath by his father's interference

in his love affair, and by the further discovery that one of his intimate friends is a spy for the Emperor. He throws off the restraint which reason has dictated, and reassuring himself with the old rationale that the end justifies the means, he seizes power. When he makes the cynical speech about Napoleon teaching revolutionists the tricks of their trade, Sceps asks,

But is this model
apt for your purpose, Highness?

To which Rudolph replies,

If it works
when it's but a trick, it should be more effective
when we mean to carry it out. We must weld the nation
in one day, in one hour. Is policy
the peculiar possession of thieves?[8]

It is a searching question—"Is policy the peculiar possession of thieves?" It is what modern man would like most to know: Is it possible to be wise as serpents and at the same time harmless as doves? Has our dramatist-prophet any answer to the question?

Not in this play. *The Masque of Kings* is a tragedy, an impressive exposé of the fallacious doctrine that freedom can be achieved by violent revolution. In good faith Rudolph proposes to use his power to grant freedom; but in his first move to seize power, in the brief march from his own to his father's apartment in the Hofburg, one man is accused, bound, humiliated, and another is killed. And Rudolph discovers at once that to men who are humiliated, and to the friends of those who are killed, the new regime is not liberation but simply another tyranny.

As soon as Franz Joseph is convinced that Rudolph actually has seized the palace and the city, he shifts ground quickly. From threatening his son he turns to instructing him how to follow through with the revolution. Franz Joseph's recommendations infuriate Rudolph, provoking him to make rash declarations which startle his followers. He commits himself to suppression, confiscation, mass executions. One of his supporters, the journalist Herr Sceps, hears with dismay that there will be censorship—for a time. It appears that there will be highhanded methods in all directions—for a time. Rudolph himself begins to see that he will be forced to act in ways which he was resolved to avoid. In a moment of despair he turns his back on those in the room and looks out of the window. Koinoff, who has been informing on the Prince, springs forward to stab Rudolph; but Franz Joseph throws himself between them and is struck down. Rudolph bends over his father, helping him to his feet.

Rudolph. Why do you risk your life
to save mine?

Franz Joseph. Why, because you've forty years
of life in you, and I have ten or twelve—
and we're alike. I shall have no other son,
but you may breed a dozen Habsburgs yet
to send the name on.

Rudolph. Sir, have you joined my rebellion
against yourself?

Franz Joseph. Why, lad, I've won! I've won!
What I want most is to leave a king behind me
such as I see you are!

Rudolph. You wanted this?
You played for it?

Franz Joseph. How often what we've wanted
comes to us in the night, a little early,
too unexpected, and we put it by,
and it never comes again. I take my way
quite happily into what darkness you prescribe,
my son, knowing now I leave behind a king
after my heart, a better than myself,
but a king, and a Habsburg king! He will chew on iron
who tries to eat you, now that your salad days
are over. When you speak you speak the words
of Wittelsbachs and fools, but when you act
then you're my son, and the long quarrel in your blood
between the Empress and myself, the quarrel
that lay in your conceiving, it's now ended,
and I shall win, by dying.

Rudolph. I shall not rule
as you have.

Franz Joseph. You'll try reforms, and then you'll learn
that all reforms are counters in the game
of government, played to get what you want;
a trick of management. I tried it too,
and found it useful. We have said goodnight—
the guard is ready, you have things in hand,
and I'm sorry to have kept you. Before you sleep

look in that little black book on your desk—
and read three words of it. I think you'll find
it's worth your time.

Rudolph. I am the thing I hate!
Among us all we've made of me the thing
I shall hate most till I die. The thing I do,
caught on this bayonet of time, and driven,
repeats in word for word and death for death,
his coronation.[9]

This is the climax. Only a swift resolution of the
action should follow this illumination. Franz Joseph's
reference to the little black book brings Mary Vetsera
forward to beg Rudolph not to look into it. But she tells
him what it is. She kept a diary when she first knew him,
reporting where they went and what they did.

And so his love, too, is blasted by disillusionment.
But there is not enough substance in the discovery and
its results to justify a third act. What Rudolph and Mary
say to each other the next morning at the hunting lodge
could have been said more effectively, without inflation,
as they face one another over the diary.

He has lost his faith, and men cannot live without
faith. And his love turned out to be a "little, dirty, cal-
culating love." Mary admits that she was shallow; but
finding that Rudolph loved her, she became something
other than she was. Not sure now that she could be
steadfast if his love were withdrawn, she shoots herself.
Her act teaches him "how to keep faith with the little
faith I have." He knows now what he must do; but,
theatrically speaking, he must do it at once. All the

dialogue of the third act—his mother's imploring him
and his father's trying to bribe him to become the thing
he despises—is repetitious and anticlimactic.

The last scene of Act II is a brilliant achievement
of the kind of double-edged action and dialogue which
Mr. Anderson likes to write: everything said being pertinent to the fiction enacted on the stage and at the same
time lighting up for the audience the modern conflicts
which the audience itself faces.

Those conflicts were rapidly resolving themselves
into just one question: Would we stand and defend our
way of life, with all its imperfections upon it? There was
no more time for hesitation, for self-reproach, for speculations about theoretical values. By 1938 something in
the way of national affirmation, some kind of declaration
of faith had become imperative.

At this juncture Maxwell Anderson turned from the
role of prophet to that of priest, from speaking to the
people regarding the fundamental character of power
and of freedom, to speaking for them in a theatrical
celebration of such principles and purposes as we then
actually possessed. Our convictions were found to be
simple indeed, matter only for a musical comedy.

Knickerbocker Holiday is a genuine expression of
the American spirit, the spirit of laughter in the face of
danger. Mr. Anderson makes no comment on our inability
to take ourselves and our world quite seriously, gives
no hint as to whether he regards our merriment as a
saving sense of humor or a possibly fatal flippancy. He
merely takes it as he finds it, and makes of it a highly
amusing farce.

In the late thirties Mr. Anderson was at the peak of his creative freedom; and *Knickerbocker Holiday*, like *The Star Wagon* and *High Tor,* is a riotous concoction of real and unreal, truth and nonsense, fact and fantasy. The play is a kind of Orwell speculation in reverse: not what our condition would be if totalitarianism should prevail in America in 1984, but a make-believe that it was tried by our founding fathers in 1647. Washington Irving is the impresario of the comedy, and interferes from time to time to keep the piece from taking a turn which might be offensive to "posterity."

The scene is New York Harbor. A new governor of the colony is expected. The occasion calls for a holiday, and a holiday calls for a hanging. Someone ventures to ask why there must be a hanging, and he is given money and told to "Hush!" This trick of literalizing abstractions is typical of the play. The dictator's "smelling" opposition is another instance.

Brom Broeck, the hero, is, of course, selected for the necessary hanging, though the council has not yet found a law by which he can be arraigned. And no one has the courage to try to arrest him, for he cannot take orders and cannot be counted on to go along quietly. Brom bargains with the council, promising to find someone for the hanging. He proposes Herr Tienhoven, who sells liquor and firearms to the Indians; and that incriminates Brom, for there is a law prescribing death for anyone bringing an accusation against a councilman. Brom decides to submit, asking only that he be hanged the old way, by the neck, which is quick and sure, rather than the modern way, by the belly.

The play continues in this idiotic vein. A complete résumé of the action is not necessary to convey its flavor. The attempted execution inevitably reminds one of *The Mikado;* and it would be something of a minor miracle if anyone writing social or political satire in musical comedy terms should succeed in avoiding the overpowering influence of Gilbert and Sullivan. Mr. Anderson does not altogether escape; it is not likely that he tried. He appears to have the grand indifference of the greatest writers with regard to mere inventiveness, appropriating whatever will serve his purpose. The castigation of immoral behavior by the dramatic device of allowing the characters to assume and parade a code exactly opposite to the ethical standards which society professes, and to do this not in the spirit of heroic defiance, or of bravado, or of titillating naughtiness, but as if it were itself a moral code—this method was not original with Mr. Anderson or with William Schwenck Gilbert. As Mr. Anderson uses it, the effect is very much like that of *The Beggar's Opera.* Like that of *The Beggar's Opera,* too, is the impression (produced by the extravagant antics) that the whole play is being improvised on the spot, from moment to moment, by the actors themselves.

The new governor of the colony pardons Brom because he was smart enough to save his own life, and then the governor declares himself dictator. But the one thing he cannot tolerate is a man unable to take orders. And he can smell opposition. He goes sniffing about until he discovers the opposition in Brom, who is then thrown into jail. Governor Stuyvesant visits Brom there and suggests that he write a book on his theories of government—so many important books have been written in jail.

In the last act Brom is released by an Indian attack. He fights the Indians and loses his friend in the struggle. Governor Stuyvesant gives Brom leave "to speak in Caesar's funeral," whereupon Brom accuses Stuyvesant of selling firearms to the Indians. Stuyvesant protests—there is no witness; and "Caesar," not waiting for a ghostly appearance, straightway rises and testifies.

Brom is once more in danger of hanging; but now he incites the council to rebellion. Just as Stuyvesant is about to man a cannon, Irving interferes to remind the actors of posterity.

Amid the rollicking nonsense there are two motifs that we are obviously expected to take seriously: the question, What is an American? and the expression, in Franklinese terms, of typical American optimism: When you hit bottom the only way out is up.

The best definition of the national character which we were able to bring forth in 1938 was that an American is "A person with a really fantastic and inexcusable aversion to taking orders, coupled with a complete abhorrence for governmental corruption and an utter incapacity for doing anything about it." Mr. Anderson knows well that Americans are pleased with this characterization of themselves. It is essentially the same as that expressed more seriously in *Valley Forge*. And the first part of the description, the inability to take orders, is

the most appealing quality which he can give to those
great rebels of his history plays, Lord Essex and Lord
Bothwell.

"There is one man in all her kingdom she fears,"
Francis Bacon says to Lord Essex, "And that man's yourself, and she has good reason to fear you/You're a man
not easily governed, a natural rebel."

Mary Stuart says to Lord Bothwell,

You have never yet
Learned how to take an order.

And he replies,

And never will—
From man or woman living, sovereign or knave,
Judge or vicegerent. I have not been conquered
And will not be. But I offer you my fealty,
And it's worth the more for that.[10]

Americans thrill to such utterances. And even the
contradiction in the second part of the description, "a
complete abhorrence for governmental corruption and
an utter incapacity for doing anything about it," we look
upon with neither chagrin nor anxiety. It seems to us an
endearing lunacy rather than any threat to our security.

In dealing with national ideals Maxwell Anderson
is at the very center of a great dramatic tradition. The
whole body of Shakespeare's chronicle plays is a ritualis-
tic celebration of England's national greatness. This celebration is present not only in the great set speeches, like
that of Gaunt in *Richard II*. It is also in the conviction,

dramatized repeatedly, that England is invincible as long as Englishmen are not divided among themselves. Strife among them often creates the danger which leads to near disaster. But Englishmen come to their senses in time to ward off the final blow. Since the uncertainty and confusion is frequently caused by a king who is not kingly, the plays turn out to be a definition of kingship, a celebration of the great British principle that England's right to a king is superior to any man's title to a throne. Shakespeare did not have to labor his point, for he was writing for a people jubilant in their recent victory over their most powerful rival, and united under a monarch who embodied and expressed the national spirit.

Mr. Anderson, to his misfortune, was obliged to write his celebration of the national ideal before its testing and its triumph. Hence he was unable to sustain the role of spokesman for the people. He found that artists, like men of other professions, have a stake in freedom, and he could not be content with turning "the best ideas current at the time" into works of art. The ideas about democracy current in America in 1938 were, in his judgment, not sound, not adequate to sustain the nation in a war of ideologies. He was constrained to play his part as a citizen as well as an artist. He tried to clarify the ideas which are basic to freedom. He claims that he had no intention of saying anything new or shocking, but he found that "when the play came out there was a good deal of critical bewilderment over the political opinions expressed in it, and not a little resentment at my definitions of government and democracy."

If we read Brom's speech at the end of Act II we may
readily understand the bewilderment and the resentment.

I guess all governments are crooked, I guess they're all vicious
and corrupt, but a democracy has the immense advantage of
being incompetent in villainy and clumsy in corruption. Now,
your tyranny's another matter—. . . It's efficiently vicious and
efficiently corrupt! They're both bad. But since we have to have
one or the other let's throw out this professional and go back
to the rotation of amateurs! Let's keep the government small
and funny, and maybe it'll give us less discipline and more
entertainment![11]

A nation preparing itself for a life-and-death struggle
with tyranny could scarcely be expected to believe it
was intending to shed its own blood for so dubious an
end as mere inefficient corruption. Yet there was more
truth in the observation than the audience realized. The
fact is the free world denied only the "corruption." We
accepted the label of "inefficient" which our enemies
fastened upon democracy. We had to admit that democracy looks inefficient. We were somewhat disconcerted
by the accusation, but we did not have time to think
the matter through. The enemy was insisting on trial by
battle; and freedom, for all its apparent inefficiency,
survived the test.

But the defenders of freedom, including their
spokesman-playwright, evidently still do not understand
why we were victorious—that a free people can defend
itself against a regimented people, not because inefficiency is stronger than regimentation, but because

individual responsibility is stronger, even with one hand tied by inefficiency, than individual irresponsibility, with both hands tied by regimentation. If we really understood this bit of fundamental wisdom, if this is what we learned from our successful resistance to totalitarianism, then Mr. Anderson should have had something quite new to say in his latest treatment of freedom and government. Yet *Barefoot in Athens* is not a great celebration of something heroic in man. What it is, exactly, is probably the most baffling question we shall encounter in our reading of Maxwell Anderson's plays.

[1] Thomas Stearns Eliot, *Selected Essays, New Edition 1950*, Harcourt Brace and Company, New York, 1950, pp. 117-118.

[2] John Mason Brown, *Two on the Aisle*, W. W. Norton, New York, 1938, pp. 208-209.

[3] *Ibid.*, p. 210.

[4] Maxwell Anderson, *Valley Forge*, in *Eleven Verse Plays*, Harcourt, Brace and Company, New York, 1940, Act I, Scene II, pp. 23-24.

[5] ———, *The Masque of Kings*, in *Eleven Verse Plays*, Act I, Scene II, p. 30.

[6] *Ibid.*, pp. 41-43.

[7] *Ibid.*, Act II, Scene II, pp. 75-76.

[8] *Ibid.*, p. 76.

[9] *Ibid.*, Act II, Scene III, pp. 109-111.

[10] ———, *Mary of Scotland*, in *Eleven Verse Plays*, Act II, Scene I, p. 100.

[11] ———, *Knickerbocker Holiday*, Anderson House, Washington, D. C., 1938, Act II, Scene II, pp. 100-101.

CHAPTER V

The Failure
of the Quest

"What Mr. Anderson has attempted," says George Jean Nathan, commenting on *Barefoot in Athens* in his book, *The Theatre in the Fifties*, "is a picture of the Greek philosopher caught in the ideational turbulence consequent upon the Spartan conquest of Athens that led to the trial for his championship of free inquiry, regarded as subversive by the political leaders of the time." Mr. Nathan assumes, as anyone would, that a play about Socrates on trial for his championship of free inquiry is intended to be a drama of ideas, and as such he finds the play a failure. On my first reading of *Barefoot in Athens* I made the same assumption and came to the same conclusion. But I cannot dismiss an Anderson play with one reading. I have found too many times that his plays improve on further acquaintance. And the more I read in this one, the more I doubt that it was intended as a drama of ideas.

Mr. Anderson knows what such drama should be. He has described it accurately and with evident admiration in *Off Broadway* in his essay on George Bernard Shaw. And if he intended to write such drama he has indeed failed. There is no "glittering debate" pursued "with a logic and a wit so flashing as often to seem superhuman." Socrates' opponents fall before his questions as if they were mortally wounded, and the reader marvels, seeing that they have only been mischievously tripped.

I do not altogether agree with Mr. Nathan's opinion that the Socrates of the play is no more than a tricky debater. Judging from Mr. Anderson's preface, that is exactly what he tried to avoid.

> More and more, as I grew older, I was troubled in reading Plato by discovering that I did not like the Socrates who continued to discourse so charmingly and so bewilderingly in the later dialogues. I didn't like him because I didn't trust him. I caught him playing tricks with words, not for fun, and not to get at the truth, but to conceal and throw dust and obfuscate.[1]

Yet he allows his hero to give just such an account of himself.

> *Socrates.* Now I was only an irresponsible ignoramus, but I began to find that I knew as much about many things as the important people did. And I began to question them and stick needles in them—and sometimes I showed them up as ignoramuses—and they were angry. And I invented a sort of question-and-answer game for getting people into corners, and my following grew larger, because there's nothing people like better than seeing public men confused and unable to answer.

I was just as unable to answer as they were, but I was asking
the questions, not answering them, and so I acquired a reputation for wisdom which I didn't deserve and don't deserve
now. . . .[2]

If Mr. Anderson was dissatisfied with Plato's Socrates, what has he done to redeem the portrait? He has
reversed the timetable, making the young Socrates the
mental prankster, taking a malicious delight in his power
to disconcert his victims. Yet even after the message
from the Delphic oracle gives Socrates a serious turn,
he still does not alter his method, though admitting its
sterility.

Socrates. . . . I have not found one man who knows what holi-
ness is, or wisdom, or courage or loyalty or faith. And I
still don't know.[3]

This is trifling. Of course he knows what faith is.
He acts on it habitually, as all men do. He calls a god a
god, and takes quite seriously the message brought him
from Apollo. He postulates at least a half dozen absolutes without defining them: truth, freedom, democracy,
that truth cannot be harmed, that certain things are
good or beautiful, that man knows nothing but ought
to seek knowledge at all times in all places. He tells
Xantippe that nothing is ever concluded. Yet when he
and his three friends had sat talking all night, in that
distant time of which he reminds Critias, they "concluded that the most valuable thing a man or a state
could have was freedom." And they further concluded
what was necessary for the preservation of freedom, and

even swore an oath that they would support democracy at all cost.

The exasperating thing about this play is that in thirty years of knocking his fellow citizens over the head, there is not one Greek in all Socrates' miracle city with enough wit to demand that he answer some questions or define the terms he uses. For drama of ideas to be at all exciting there must be someone in the play who comes close to being a match for the protagonist; but Socrates has it all his own way. When he asks Metelos at the trial, "Do you believe the truth can do harm?" and "Do you believe free discussion can do harm?" Metelos stands meekly answering "No," while the reader, far from being entertained by a quick thrust and counter-thrust of keen minds at strife, is vexed that the most obvious retorts do not occur to Metelos. Socrates has already admitted in the open court that there was never any real discussion, that he asked all the questions. And his only defense of his interminable questioning is, "It was our way to question everything." To say, "It was our way," is not to say, and certainly not to prove, it was a good way. "It has been my fixed principle that the uncovering of truth could do no harm," he says, knowing that all will agree. And then he adds, as if it followed logically, which it doesn't, "I have believed that questioning could injure only what is false." The assumption is that questioning is the way to uncover truth; but nothing in the evidence, including his own testimony, indicates that his little game was bringing truth to light. And something has been injured which was not false. Three of the most intelligent, most promising young men of Athens have been corrupted. One of them, Critias, accuses Socrates of the mischief; but he does not live to bring his testimony to the trial.

It is the trial, of course, the central place which it has in the play, and the importance which Socrates attaches to it, which leads the reader to expect a drama of ideas. When news is brought of the indictment, Socrates is jubilant.

Xantippe. I knew this would happen!

Socrates. I didn't. It's better than I could have hoped for. They've delivered themselves into my hands. They are fools in an argument, all of them.

After some further comment from others Socrates adds:

It's a heaven-sent opportunity to defend my way of life in open court. And Athens will laugh them into exile. In any other city there'd be doubt of the outcome. Here, among the clear heads of the merry Greeks it's unalloyed good fortune. I'll win and they'll pay and never hear the end of it.[4]

Later, when the charge is renewed, his zest for the fight is still keen.

Socrates. . . . I look forward to this trial as an athlete looks forward to the race he has longed for, as a wrestler looks forward to the bout for which all his life has been a training. All my life I've been accused of things and I've never been able to answer back. Day after tomorrow is my day![5]

All this prepares us for a brilliant display of intellectual fireworks. But the merry Greeks, after the Spartan occupation, are no longer merry; and a debate with fools, if they are fools, is a precarious venture under any circumstances. When Anytas twists into proof of impiety the perfectly acceptable analogy by which Socrates sought to describe his belief in the gods through his acknowledged belief in the demigods, he is doing exactly what a person of no intellectual power would do; and the tragic outcome of the play is clearly foreshadowed.

But Socrates is not doing much better when he equates "believing in" with "knowing much about," even though he has tried to forestall objection by claiming that words do not have fixed meanings, but shift about. He believes in several things, though he protests, "All my wisdom is in knowing how little I know. None of my questions has been answered, none of the definitions I sought has been found."

To demonstrate his faith he says,

... We live our lives, it seems to me, in such mystery and darkness that I was quick to take the one hint I thought might have come my way from a god, the answer made by the Delphic Apollo to a question about myself. Since that answer I have continued to seek, sometimes gaily, sometimes ironically, but always seriously, for somebody wiser than I am. Perhaps I was wrong, but this is the closest I have ever come to hearing a mandate from any god, and I wished to do as the god directed.[6]

The fact is, the god directed nothing to be done. Socrates' answer may demonstrate his faith, but it does not demonstrate very great intellectual power. The only genuine clash of thought is that between Lycon and Socrates.

Lycon goes straight to the heart of the matter. Socrates is not on trial for his good intentions, but for his acts. Whether or not truth can do harm, harm has been done and appears to have been done by Socrates. All of the traitors have been his pupils. Truth must have been wanting somewhere: in the man, or in the method. Lycon says, the skill he taught was a "devilish ingenuity."

We recall the testimony of Critias:

Critias. Whatever I believe you taught me! What I do you taught me to do!

Socrates. Indeed?

Critias. Did you not teach us to question our gods, our laws, our customs, and the very meaning of the words we used?

Socrates. It was our way to question everything.

Critias. And did we find anything sure?

Socrates. Nothing sure, worse luck.

Critias. Then why not murder, why not rob, why not take what you want where you find it? There are no rules!

Socrates' answer is good, but it comes twenty-five years too late.

Socrates. But while we are at it, Critias, should we not also question the value of murder, the value of blood money, the value of high office in the state illegally attained, before we destroy all we have to possess them?[7]

Socrates' answer to Lycon is even better. It is in fact, one of the best things he says: he did not choose for the young men who learned their skill in debate from him. For himself he chose to fight for Athens and to walk her streets seeking the truth.

Yet he does not sustain this level of argument. When Lycon says no belief will bear examination, a tree cannot live if its roots are exposed, Socrates thinks he is blasting the idea when he says, "This would be a very convenient rule for a tyrant or a dictator who did not wish to be examined, of course." It evidently escapes his notice that he has just defended his own learning method by the same logic: the questioning method is good; his pupils misused it. He has acknowledged that good things are subject to abuse and perversion.

There is a terrible irony in what Socrates says about evidence. He has flashed out in anger because Lycon has accused him of hating Athens. He loves Athens.

Socrates. And the thing I have loved most about my city is its freedom, its willingness to look at all the evidence there is and live in the same world with it.

Lycon. Even if the evidence destroys it?

Socrates. The evidence will not destroy a free city, Lycon. Far from destroying it, the truth will make and keep it free. A despotism dies of the truth, a democracy lives by it![8]

Once more his words have shifted about. Evidence and truth are not synonymous, at least not in court. His own question-and-answer game did not uncover the truth. And the little question-and-answer game which his accusers are now playing with him in court likewise does not get at the truth. And the evidence, such as it is, destroys him, though it is true that he loves Athens and meant to do good. He had been strictly honest in regard to the trial, refusing to resort to any tricks in order to influence the jury.

Socrates. You see, Crito, I am accused of being the kind of man who corrupts and falsifies and distorts and destroys. Now if I am that kind of man I should be put out of the way. But how can the jury tell what kind of man I am if I go before them speaking words that are not mine and hiding behind a crying wife and children?[9]

However, it is too late now for honesty and candor and protestations of love for Athens. Socrates is at last a public figure with a reputation which others may envy. If men like to see other men confused and unable to answer, what more exhilarating spectacle than seeing Socrates entangled in his own words! He is led to declare that if he had to choose between Athens and the search for truth, he would choose truth. Then the trap is sprung.

Lycon. And so his allegiance is not to our city, but to the truth, the phantom truth that he has never found.[10]

And Socrates is found guilty.

Socrates had found the truth but he did not know it, the truth that the life of man is so mysterious, so full of uncertainties, that nothing but the most absolute faith can sustain it. He was mischievous as a teacher because he communicated to his pupils all his doubts without finding a game by which to communicate also the faith by which he himself actually lived. That is his tragedy. He made the fatal mistake of restricting his concept of truth to that which could be encompassed by reason alone. Mr. Anderson says of Shaw, who is his "hero as thinker": "He has discovered that in a world where no man knows anything surely the man who assumes a conviction can be king." From certain correspondences between the essay on Shaw and *Barefoot in Athens*—in words as well as ideas—one gets the impression that it is just such a hero Mr. Anderson intended to portray in Socrates. But the play is an artistic failure because Socrates is not aware that he has assumed convictions. He takes no account of the fact in any of his conversations about truth. And just at the point where he should have been confronted with his error, the emphasis shifts from him to the citizens of Athens, and the play takes a new direction, seeming to promise a tragedy of democracy.

By a *deus ex machina* Socrates is rescued by appeal to history and turned into a martyr. Though the entire development of the play up to the announcement of the verdict is an exposé of the failure of dialectic, Socrates is allowed to triumph through a few well-chosen absolutes which his dialectic has never recognized, and the citizens of Athens are convicted of a gross injustice in condemning a wise and good man, and of deserting the democratic ideal in rejecting freedom of thought.

The reader is constantly aware of this possible meaning. All the tragic potential of democracy is present and operating throughout the play. The factors which stand out most clearly are those we have already noted in earlier plays: that democracy is a wonderfully dangerous collection of contradictions, that there is apparently no limit to the evil it can contain and yet survive; that "When a man is free he is free to choose wrong or right"; and especially that there is some necessary connection between stupidity and freedom. Illustrative of the first item is Socrates' rhapsody on Athens in the opening scene of the play.

Socrates. . . . I wish I could tell you what I feel for this city, Xantippe! This Athens, a gathering of slaves and free men, of artists and unprincipled traitors, of staggering genius and sure-footed dolts, of soaring altars to the gods built with stolen money, of level-headed madmen who speak like their own goddess of wisdom and then filch the gold fringe from that goddess's image, a pack of poets who are generals, and of generals who grow rich by selling their prisoners, of men who are paragons of virtue and evil, who have done everything a man should do, and also everything he should not! A hive of inspired and brainy and reckless idiots, who love the arts more than money, and fame more than the arts, and politics more than all three! How they have done it I don't know, and they don't, but they've built such a city here as the gods must have been thinking of when they first made men—a city drowned in sunlight and dancing and music and wisdom and deviltry, and crowned with the mystic marbles of the Parthenon![11]

Expressions of the last factor, that there is a necessary

relationship between stupidity and freedom, occur throughout the play. The following bit of dialogue is typical.

Pausanias. Is this what you call democracy?

Critias. This is democracy. Have you had enough of it? May I change the subject now?

Pausanias. Yes. But democracy is as stupid as I am.

Socrates. As stupid as all of us put together, O King. But free.[12]

Yet a tragedy of democracy also fails to materialize. The author is not willing to allow the audience to experience the terror of a people's tragedy. Hence, what might have been a very good tragic effect is dissipated in flattery and extenuation.

Socrates. Then I'm found guilty.

Magis. It seems so.

Socrates. Why, the jury which has been silent throughout has been thinking in its silence. And the outcome depends on the silent jury, not on us who were talking. I thought it would go the other way.

Magis. I thought so, too.

Socrates. I thought it had gone the other way.
(*He looks slowly round at the crowd*)
I have not known my city then. More than half of these faces that look up at me are the faces of men who have said,

"No more for Socrates." I've lived too long, perhaps, and you grow tired of me. Well, it's your right to grow weary of any man.[13]

This flattery of the people is shocking. There is no reason to suppose the jury had been doing any serious thinking. They were bitter. They had suffered under a foreign tyrant. It is quite likely they were looking for a scapegoat.

Certainly it is nobody's right to grow weary of any man to the point of putting him to death for no better reason than that they are weary of him. Again the words of Socrates are shifting about in meaning. The citizens of a democracy do not have the right to do wrong. What they have is the power. They may abuse their power as other rulers do. But might does not make right in a democracy any more than in a monarchy or a dictatorship. There is no escaping the moral law by recourse to numbers. Power is corrupting, as corrupting to a group as to an individual. But Mr. Anderson cannot bring himself to allow his play to reveal this truth. He has a stake in freedom. He wishes to keep a free people believing in themselves and in their institutions; and evidently he is not altogether persuaded that the truth can do no harm.

Still, in this play as in *The Feast of Ortolans*, a kind of absolute meaning emerges. It is, in its confusion of unresolved contradictions, in its exhibition of man's inability to look squarely at facts without falling into suicidal cynicism, and especially in its myth of the romantic hope of solving major problems by the application of perfume in just the right spots—in all these the play is an image of the mind of our time.

[1] Maxwell Anderson, *Barefoot in Athens,* William Sloane Associates, Inc., New York, 1951, p. viii.

[2] *Ibid.,* Act II, Scene II, p. 72.

[3] *Ibid.,* p. 73.

[4] *Ibid.,* Act I, Scene I, pp. 13-14.

[5] *Ibid.,* Act II, Scene I, p. 66.

[6] *Ibid.,* Act II, Scene II, p. 78.

[7] *Ibid.,* Act I, Scene II, pp. 32-33.

[8] *Ibid.,* Act II, Scene II, p. 83.

[9] *Ibid.,* Act II, Scene I, p. 66.

[10] *Ibid.,* Act II, Scene II, p. 84.

[11] *Ibid.,* Act I, Scene I, p. 11.

[12] *Ibid.,* Act I, Scene II, p. 25.

[13] *Ibid.,* Act II, Scene II, p. 86.

CHAPTER VI

The War Plays

It is in the war plays of the past thirty years that the reader will find the sharpest and truest image of the mind of our time. There can be no denying that "To fight or not to fight?" has been the central question of the twentieth century; and the four distinct phases of the changing attitudes on that issue which have succeeded one another so precipitously are all clearly reflected in the plays of Maxwell Anderson. Historians of contemporary drama, in summing up the development, have generally failed to recognize the second phase, because it did not produce its own plays but appears only as incidental comment in plays on other themes.

The first period, represented by *What Price Glory*, is the period of deglamourizing war, the blasting of glory, honor, and patriotism. *What Price Glory*, written in collaboration with Laurence Stallings, presents a squad of marines in the midst of the toughest fighting of the First World War, and the quarrel between a

98

very tough top sergeant and an equally tough captain over a little camp follower. For the first time in theatrical history soldiers on the stage were not romantic and not heroic. In his own note on the play Maxwell Anderson claimed realism as a conscious purpose, and focused attention on the profanity as the peculiar stamp of that realism.

> *What Price Glory* is a play of war as it is, not as it has been presented theatrically for thousands of years. The soldiers talk and act much as soldiers the world over. The speech of men under arms is universally and consistently interlarded with profanity. Oaths mean nothing to a soldier save a means to obtain emphasis. He uses them in place of more polite adjectives.
>
> The authors of *What Price Glory* have attempted to reproduce this mannerism along with other general atmosphere they believe to be true. In a theatre where war has been lied about, romantically, effectively—and in a city where the war play has usually meant sugary dissimulation—*What Price Glory* may seem bold. The audience is asked to bear with certain expletives which, under other circumstances, might be used for melodramatic effect, but herein are employed because the mood and truth of the play demand their employment.[1]

It is likely to seem a little surprising to a reader of the mid-century that the characteristic profanity of the soldier should have loomed so large in the initial impact of the play. That it does surprise us is evidence that the battle for realism is won. But among the principal critics of this play only Joseph Wood Krutch observes that the matter goes deeper than surface realism, that profanity is only one manifestation of the

general dislocation of values, of which lewd speech of
all kinds, excessive drinking, and open fornication are
others. No one seems to be aware of the simple fact
that the violent language is an effort to equalize the
pressures outside by a violence from within, that the
most decent young man is likely to resort to profanity
in war as one equalizes physical pressure by swallow-
ing in an elevator or an airplane. The observation hardly
applies to such men as Captain Flagg and Sergeant
Quirt. But if Mr. Anderson had realized this distinction, his efforts to achieve verisimilitude in his plays
of the Second World War might have been more successful, or at least the profanity might have had less
the appearance of being turned on and off as the author
remembered or forgot to remember that the audience
expects it.

The most important point with regard to *What
Price Glory* is the one which Professor Krutch dis-
cusses at some length in both of his books on the
modern theatre; namely, that the play is classical rather
than revolutionary. The distinction is that between
"playwriting as an art" and "playwriting as a method
of changing the intellectual atmosphere." Or, as he sums
up the matter later, the playwrights of the classical
stamp show "a tendency to be more interested in dis-
playing human life against a certain background of
moral assumptions than in presenting the argumenta-
tive defense of those assumptions." To put it still another way, "The difference is nevertheless real between
the play which exploits the emotional consequences
of an attitude whose existence is taken for granted and

the play which undertakes to define or to win acceptance for the attitudes which alone can give its story
the meaning which the author intended."

> In *What Price Glory* Laurence Stallings and Maxwell
> Anderson wrote a melodramatic farce about war which
> took it for granted that the audience was ready to think
> about soldiers, not in terms of any *dulce et decorum
> est* . . . , but in terms of a "modern" disillusion with the
> whole concept of military glory.[2]

Writing of the play at the time of its initial per-
formance in 1924, Professor Krutch had observed that
the significant thing about war, to the dramatists, "is
not death and destruction but the way of life which it
develops," an "anti-civilization," he calls it.

> What effect, if any, the piece may have had as propa-
> ganda against war is not a question necessary to ask
> as part of the present discussion. The authors were not
> inventing a new morality calculated to shock and outrage
> a public unaware that any new morality was called for.
> They hardly carried the *thinking* of their audience further
> than the audience itself, already cynical on the subject
> of military glory, had already carried it. What they did
> do was take advantage of the fact that a play which
> had never been written—which until about that time
> could not have been written—was now possible: a play
> which assumed that the psychology of the soldier could
> be interpreted in terms such as those they chose and
> still remain immediately comprehensible. The great and
> instantaneous success of the play is itself proof of the
> fact that its moral assumptions were those which a large
> public was ready to accept even if it had never before
> accepted them so explicitly.[3]

Not only is the question of propaganda value of no importance in discussing the intrinsic merits of the play; it also was not particularly important to the public which saw the play in 1924. The mood of the country in the early twenties was merely cynical. But the anti-war movement, the second phase in the changing attitude, developed very rapidly. By the end of the twenties and in the early thirties church and university groups and clubs of all kinds were holding peace conferences and publishing resolutions outlawing war. There was no anxiety. The mood was serious but confident. War was costly, futile, and therefore stupid. It was no longer necessary to deglamourize it and not yet necessary to dread it. The writers merely dismissed it in well-turned phrases calculated to override any lingering doubts in the minds of the unsophisticated. In *Gods of the Lightning* (1928) we read,

Salter. In 1917 you left your home to avoid the draft, didn't you?

Capraro. Yes.

Salter. You opposed the war?

Capraro. It was a war for business, a war for billions of dollars, murder of young men for billions.

* * *

Salter. Do you honor the flag?

Capraro. I did before I came to this country. Now I know it is like all the other flags. They are all the same. When we are young boys we look on a flag and believe it is the flag

of liberty and happy people—and now I know it is a flag to
carry when the old men kill the young men for billions.[4]

The tone in *Elizabeth the Queen* (1930) is somewhat more restrained.

Elizabeth. I am no coward either.
It requires more courage not to fight than to fight
When one is surrounded by hasty hot-heads, urging
Campaigns in all directions.

In *Valley Forge* (1934) the Congressmen represent
the view that wars are instigated for money and fought
by dupes.

Harvie. ...
It has not yet been brought to a vote in Congress—
nor did we wish it published, but this is true.
There are those among us who know that a war is worth
what it brings on the exchange, no more. And when
your stock is going down, it's best to sell
before it goes to nothing.

Stirling. What's that? What's that?

Harvie. Why, I'll say it again. A war, my friend,
is a tactical expedient to gain
certain political ends. Those ends being proved
impossible, the war's without excuse,
and should be pushed no further than need be
to gain an advantageous peace.

Stirling. You say it,
and I must believe you've said it, but, death of God,
is this like any other war?

Harvie. The same,
or much the same.

Washington. Sir, I should have supposed
you'd notify me, before negotiations
were begun with the enemy.

Harvie. There was thought of it,
but you and your army have so much of the hot-head
in your composition, it was believed unwise
to open the subject. Besides, there was always doubt
what reply we'd get from the English, and it seemed best
not to call off our dogs till we were sure
we had no need for them.

Washington. Your dogs, you say!

Harvie. Nay, that's a figure.

Washington. Not one I'm inclined to relish![5]

Washington, Stirling, and Varnum try to maintain that
this war is different from others. But the sentiments
of Lucifer Tench hark back to Captain Flagg and Sergeant Quirt: soldiers fight for their pay and have what
fun they can snatch.

Tench. ...   I'm not a pious man;
I'm a soldier, as Varnum says he is, and a soldier's business
is to fight when he has to, run away when he can,
eat if he can get it, drink as much as there is,
and stay alive.[6]

                          *   *   *

Tench. You leave us, lady?

Mary. Broken-hearted.

Tench. You should have come to me.
I mend these broken hearts.

Mary. Now I believe you.

Tench. This is a poor excuse for a war we're in,
anyway—why, to mend a broken heart I'd leave
at the drop of an eyelash—but, damn it, duty calls,
and, God, we're hounds for duty![7]

The third period was abruptly inaugurated in 1936
by the appearance of three plays, *Idiot's Delight* by
Robert Sherwood, *Bury the Dead* by Irwin Shaw, and
Johnny Johnson by Paul Green. Cynicism had given
place to bitterness and rebellion, because war, from
being a painful memory, had become a definite threat,
not to be laughed or legislated out of existence.

Maxwell Anderson held out longer than his fellow
playwrights. His comment in 1937 (*High Tor*) was
still "There's no hill worth a man's peace."

The Indian. It's an old question,
one I heard often talked of round the fire
when the hills and I were younger. Then as now
the young braves were for keeping what was ours
whatever it cost in blood. And they did try,
but when they'd paid their blood, and still must sell,
the price was always less than what it was
before their blood was paid.

Van. Well, that may be.

The Indian. I wish now I had listened when they spoke
their prophecies, the sachems of the tents;
they were wiser than I knew. Wisest of all,

Iachim, had his camp here on this Tor
before the railroad came. I saw him stand
and look out toward the west, toward the sun dying,
and say, "Our god is now the setting sun,
and we must follow it. For other races,
out of the east, will live here in their time,
one following another. Each will build
its cities, and its monuments to gods
we dare not worship. Some will come with ships,
and some with wings, and each will desecrate
the altars of the people overthrown,
but none will live forever. Each will live
its little time, and fly before the feet
of those who follow after." Let them come in
despoiling, for a time is but a time
and these will not endure. This little hill,
let them have the little hill, and find your peace
beyond, for there's no hill worth a man's peace
while he may live and find it.[8]

By 1939 Mr. Anderson had accepted the challenge
of the coming struggle, and so strong was his recoil
that nothing less than a hill to be defended could
suffice to make plain his reversal of opinion.

Yet *Key Largo* is not thesis-ridden. It is a great
play, as I hope I shall be able to demonstrate. Who
does not feel the terror of King McCloud's dilemma?

Once having saved my life
by slipping away, there never came a time
when I could say to myself, make a stand here.

He is afraid of his traitor brain, too skillful at finding
excuses. We of the twentieth century know that traitor
brain—everything "sicklied o'er with the pale cast of

thought." Joseph Wood Krutch says of the soldiers in *What Price Glory*: ʄWhen life becomes as painful and as precarious as theirs was, then the human need to make life justify itself becomes desperately acute." That is the desperate need which Mr. Anderson has dramatized again and again in his plays of modern life. Modern man, having discovered that men have been giving their lives time out of mind for hills that were not worth the price, has come to look sharply at every object, wondering if it may be counterfeit. In the past men magnified the value of the objects for which they died, and so the dying was glorious.ʃWe have come to see that it is the little things in life that really matter, that make life sweet and desirable; but we cannot reconcile ourselves to dying for little things. And when nothing seems worth dying for, it also, somehow, comes to seem not worth living for.

Mr. Anderson's hero has stated the appalling predicament with such devastating accuracy and force that we cry out with Alegre, in what amounts to a prayer,

Answer him, father, answer,
because it sounds like truth.

The talk that King McCloud and Alegre and d'Alcala have while they await the return of the sheriff and Murillo is no theoretical discussion of the values or the futility of life. It is sheer drama. King faces the ultimate choice, and he cannot escape it. The great utterances are as great as those in *Elizabeth the Queen*, yet the scene and the problem are contemporary.

The plot is one of the best of Mr. Anderson's many good plots. All things work together for a perfect complication and climax, but with nothing of the patness of the well-made play.

Key Largo has a prologue which is as vital to the play as if it were a first act; yet its distance in time and place as well as the "pastness" of its action in relation to the central situation of the play justify the distinction. On a hilltop in northern Spain in the last days of the Civil War four young Americans, on outpost duty, learn from their leader, King McCloud, that the war is lost, that the army is falling back, leaving them to hold the ridge. King is going to take them out. He has no belief in the sacredness of a lost cause. The men had already begun to have doubts about their venture, having discovered that the fight is not

a clean,
Armageddon battle, all the beasts of hell
against the angels of light.

But they recall their reasons for volunteering, and all but King decide that "the original proposition remains unchanged." There are no heroics. The language is without swagger, and equally without false modesty.

Victor. Yes, but if I die
then I know men will never give in;
then I'll know there's something in the race
of men, because even I had it, that hates injustice
more than it wants to live.—Because even I had it—
and I'm no hero.—And that means the Hitlers
and the Mussolinis always lose in the end—

force loses in the long run, and the spirit wins,
whatever spirit is. Anyway it's the thing
that says it's better to sit here with the moon
and hold them off while I can. If I went with you
I'd never know whether the race was turning
down again, to the dinosaurs—this way
I keep my faith. In myself and what men are.
And in what we may be.[9]

King deserts, is captured, and fights through the
rest of the war on Franco's side; and then returns to
America to be pursued by the Furies.

He is driven to make a pilgrimage to tell his story
to the family of each of his dead comrades. He thinks
a man has a right to live, but his demon won't have it
that way. The demon insists,

Tell your tale to them
and if one answers, yes, it was well done,
lift up your head and go on.

He comes at last to Key Largo, where Victor's father
and sister have a tourist resort. He tells them his story.
He could have saved the men. Why should he feel
guilty that they would not follow him? He shouldn't,
Alegre answers. Then he confesses why he feels guilty.
He fought with the enemy.

King. Just so they wouldn't kill me.
Something broke inside me. My nerve, maybe.
I was willing to eat dirt and be damned
if I could live. I ate dirt, and I'm damned.

D'Alcala does not know what to say. Then King

rushes on to still another confession. He has come here
with a desperate hope, because Victor had once told
him that a man could go to Alegre, his sister, with a
man's crime and be forgiven. He has dared to love her.
He asks nothing. She answers,

Why must you tell me?
About this betrayal—and then about—this love?
Why should you tell me, and make me live through it, too?
How could a woman love you?

But she says in the end, "Don't go yet." And
d'Alcala says,

Stay if you will. If you stay
it's safer for my daughter.
We're alone here and beset.

"Then I am wanted," he exclaims. It is the first
ray of hope that has struck through the darkness of his
despair.

D'Alcala and Alegre are harassed by the gambler
Murillo, who has moved into their resort, is ruining
their business, and cannot be dislodged because he
pays the county machine for protection.

King's first opportunity to make a stand is in defying
Murillo, who demands that King return the money he
won in the gambling game. He offers some resistance,
but is easily overcome. The power of this story lies in
the fact that we sympathize with King McCloud in his
failures. We agree, certainly, that it is not worth a
man's life to defend thirty dollars taken in a gambling
game.

Act II opens on a quiet scene within the house. King is sleeping on a couch. Alegre and her father are talking. D'Alcala, who lost his sight in an earlier struggle in Spain, is wondering if his sacrifice was to any purpose.

They are expecting two Indians who have promised to assist them in their efforts to oust the gamblers. A man has been murdered and his body sunk in the bay. D'Alcala has instructed the Indians to find the body, disencumber it from its weights, and let it float to be found by the police. The Indians come, report that they have done as d'Alcala directed, and ask for an old boat in which to escape. They, like King, have been trapped in a lost cause. They were picked up on a vagrancy charge when escaping from an Indian reservation to return to their tribe in the Everglades. They are now escaping from the road gang; and it is the head of the road gang who has been murdered by Murillo.

Murillo has sent word to d'Alcala that he intends to move into the house and that King is to get out. When Murillo arrives, d'Alcala tries to pass King off as his son Victor. At first, this seems to be a successful tactic, but it later turns out to be another trap for King. The sheriff comes with word that a body has been washed ashore. He will try to pin the murder on the escaped Indians. But also he remembers that there is an old charge against Victor d'Alcala and will hold King to his claim of being Victor.

Alegre tells the sheriff where he will find the Indians, and the sheriff takes Murillo with him to make

the search. While they are out, King is confronted
once more with the necessity of making a stand. Alegre
tells him she could not decide whether he or the Indians
should have to face the charge, but she will support
him in whatever he says.

There follows the magnificent passage already alluded to, in which King states the case for absolute
pessimism and d'Alcala for absolute faith. It is one of
the best things Maxwell Anderson has written, great
in its independent validity, greatest for its dramatic
appropriateness. Yet for all its force of statement and
the beauty and fitness of its imagery, the reader will
not receive the full impact of its greatness until he
comes upon it with all the burden of King's long struggle
upon him and with the sharp awareness that the sheriff
will return with the Indians almost before the thought
is completed. The young man who has failed so many
times will face once more the choice of giving or saving
his life.

The entire passage (pages 106 to 114) is too long
for quotation. I cite only as examples of the thought
and style two excerpts from d'Alcala's answer.

                                    And that's our challenge—
to find ourselves in this desert of dead light-years,
blind, all of us, in a kingdom of the blind,
living by appetite in a fragile shell
of dust and water; yet to take this dust
and water and our range of appetites
and build them toward some vision of a god
of beauty and unselfishness and truth—
could we ask better of the mud we are

than to accept the challenge, and look up
and search for god-head?[10]

Over and over again the human race
climbs up out of the mud, and looks around,
and finds that it's alone here; and the knowledge
hits it like a blight—and down it goes
into the mud again.
Over and over again we have a hope
and make a religion of it—and follow it up
till we're out on the topmost limb of the tallest tree
alone with our stars—and we don't dare to be there,
and climb back down again.
It may be that the blight's on the race once more—
that they're all afraid—and fight their way to the ground.
But it won't end in the dark. Our destiny's
the other way. There'll be a race of men
who can face even the stars without despair,
and think without going mad.[11]

King discovers that Alegre has had his picture;
and she confesses that she had fallen in love with the
man he was when he was the hero of the adventure
which took her brother to Spain. He looks at the picture
and recalls what kind of man he was. Then he realizes
what happened to him.

King. Yes. I did die in Spain.
And maybe this was what I came looking for,
this picture of the athlete who died young,
the portrait of one dead. I came a long way to get it
and tried to stay away, but now I have it
and I'll know what to do.
And yet it's unfair somehow.

Alegre. Is it unfair?

King. It doesn't come to us all. It comes to many
in certain generations, comes to only a few
in others; and it says, if you want to live
you must die now—this instant—or the food
you eat will rot at your lips, and the lips you kiss
will turn to stone, and the very ground you tread
will curl up under your footsteps like a snake
and hiss behind you.—Yet if you're chosen out,
or choose yourself, and go out to die, you die
forever after, and that's farther away
than one can say in light-years;—and the thing
you die for is as far away as that.
You die to bring about a race of men
who'll walk the heavens on a rope of sines
and cosines, looking like Wells' Martian polyp,
and operating on the womb of night
with a long sharp equation. It's no fun
to perish in your own person, when you're young,
for this remote eventuality—
even if it were attractive, which it's not;
and so in the last analysis one dies
because it's part of the bargain he takes on
when he agrees to live.—A man must die
for what he believes—if he's unfortunate
enough to have to face it in his time—
and if he won't then he'll end up believing
in nothing at all—and that's death, too.[12]

When the sheriff and Murillo return, King is able
to make his stand.

To turn from *Key Largo* to *Candle in the Wind* is
to turn from deeply moving drama to a kind of thin,

high-pitched lyricism which leaves the reader cold. Neither of the announced themes, that we can win by faith, and that it is good to fight alone, is embodied in character and action.

The enveloping situation of the play is the Nazi occupation of Paris, and the story is concerned with the prolonged efforts of an American girl, an actress, to secure the release of her fiancé from a Nazi prison. The details are quite credible, and the structure of the story is designed so as to produce an effect of suspense. Yet that effect is thwarted by other elements. The action moves too slowly. The tone and scale of the play convey an effect of attrition. There is a certain appropriateness to the content in such an effect, but it is not an effect which the reader welcomes. It does not exalt as do pity and terror.

We cannot sympathize with the leading actors because we never get inside them. We see but we do not feel what is going on. The girl, Madeline, acts throughout the play on absolute faith. In the first act it is a mystical faith—except for the language, right out of the Middle Ages. In the last act it is completely rational. But how an American actress of the twentieth century came by the first, and how she got from the first to the second, we do not know. It is easy to believe she could have come to the conclusion she does from the experiences she has been through, but we do not see this happen; and so we read her final defiance, not as the moving climax to a passionate struggle—there has been no passion at all—but simply as a rather good statement of a rational faith.

Erfurt. Take a last look about you at your free world! I have not yet spoken the word that will shut you up, but when I do speak it I will not take it back!

Madeline. I came into this fight tardily and by chance, and unwilling. I never thought to die young, or for a cause. But now that I've seen you close, now that I know you, I'd give my life gladly to gain one half inch against you! And I'll never again be worth so much against you as I am now, if you arrest me here this evening. If you think you have anything to gain by it, arrest me, imprison me, put a final end to me! It will be known! And it will not be easy to explain! Berlin will not thank you! Lash out and give the order if you're not afraid!

Erfurt. It is true that it is not expedient to arrest you now. But give me your passport. You are now a prisoner in France. (*She gives him her passport.*)
We take our enemies one at a time, and your country is last on the list. But your time will come.

Madeline. Yes. We shall expect you and be ready for you. In the history of the world, there have been many wars between men and beasts. And the beasts have always lost, and men have won.[13]

Schoen, the Nazi lieutenant, comes to an even more interesting conclusion, also without our knowing how it happens.

Schoen. Is it so easy to break with all you've ever known? To thrust your neck under the axe? I have seen too many executions. But I have come to the end of this quarrel with myself. This quarrel over whether it is better to be what you are and die for it, or to be what they would have you, and live. Perhaps I have found a sort of courage.

Madeline. Where will you go?

Schoen. You must not worry about me, I have my own private war to fight. But, however it goes, not everything is lost. For I am a soldier against what I hate, and it's good to fight alone.[14]

We feel distinctly cheated by being denied the progress of that long quarrel with himself which has ended in the discovery that it is good to fight alone. The motif of loneliness has echoed and re-echoed through the plays of Maxwell Anderson. Readers hearing the anguished cry again and again have concluded that the author is a pessimist. Nothing could be farther from the truth. Mr. Anderson is not a pessimist though he is too honest and courageous to deny or minimize the inescapable loneliness of every human existence. Believing that life is fundamentally tragic is not the same thing as believing it to be fundamentally evil. It is the latter which constitutes philosophic pessimism.

That Maxwell Anderson is not a pessimist is clear from what he has said in his critical essays as well as in many of his plays. It is his own answer to despair which he puts into the mouth of d'Alcala in the passage already quoted. He sees clearly, as few in our century have seen, that "No man is fit to live who has not found something for which he will gladly die."

But he sees this only as it applies to the moral crises of persons in what are ordinarily thought of as their private concerns. Either he does not perceive or is unwilling to face its bearing upon the choices and actions of men in their group desires and endeavors. Hence the dramas of democracy lack the moral grandeur of the great personal tragedies. The failures of democracy are not tragic or potentially tragic. They are merely ludicrous or disgusting, and he castigates them in brilliant satire. But always in satire the critic and the reader who shares the critic's point of view can remain aloof. The failures of American business, American justice, American government are not our failures. The author dares to say, at a safe distance from our involvement in an actual war, that free men must recognize the failures of democracy as their own failures.

But he does not help us to recognize that fact; for when our failures lead us once more into war, to an action our national conscience has condemned, to a method we have utterly rejected and sworn never again to adopt, he turns his eyes away. That the price of integrity may be self-sacrifice he can face for the individual but not for the nation. Elizabeth, Mary, Rudolph, King McCloud, must acknowledge how much of their tragedies have been of their own making; a great queen must face her tragic error, a great people must be spared the recognition scene which the author has declared to be the "essence of tragedy." Madeline and Schoen accept the necessity of dying for what they believe, but all ironic complexity has been carefully removed from the drama. The conflict is a "war between men and beasts." It is the Armageddon battle which only two years before Mr. Anderson had declared to be impossible.

Of course the playwright's precipitous reversal of opinion was not an isolated phenomenon. His plays reflect the attitude of the public for which they were written. That there was some sense of failure is apparent in the note of wistfulness which pervades the war plays. We went sadly into the war. But being in it, the need to make life justify itself was once more urgent. Mr. Anderson's justification, that the simple values need not be exaggerated to be worth the cost, is only faintly suggested in *The Eve of St. Mark,* is stated—overstated—but not dramatized in *Storm Operation.*

The central scene of *The Eve of St. Mark* is the one in which the young couple try to make love and discover that lovers need a house of their own. It is very simple, very touching. Nothing here is overdone. It must have been this scene which won from Brooks Atkinson the phrase "poignant sympathy." But since all questions of moral responsibility for the lovers' predicament are excluded from the play, the effect, which might have been tragic, is merely pathetic.

The play also contains one of the best comedy scenes Maxwell Anderson has written, that in the Moon Bow Restaurant (Act I, Scene IV), in which the hero and another American soldier try to divert themselves with a couple of miraculously stupid girls called Lil and Sal.

The play as a whole is unsatisfactory. "Rueful yet heroic" is the phrase in which the drama critic John Gassner characterizes it. Rueful it certainly is, but nothing so sentimental could be called heroic. It must have been written in great haste, for it delivers without qualification the lyrical idealism which is our only recourse when laughter fails us. The unalleviated purity of sentiment and conduct is embarrassing to look upon.

Storm Operation is too obviously propaganda to be interesting drama. We are really such fundamentally

decent folk, it says, we would never get involved in a
dirty business like war without being drafted into it.
But if a job has to be done—even a dirty job—we are
the ones who can do it.

Peter. I know how I got here. I got drafted, the same as the
rest of you. I didn't want to be a soldier. Nobody did, only we
knew the job had to be done, and we had to do it. And the
only way to fight a war is to make the other fellow so Goddam
sorry he picked on us that he'll never want to do it again.
And the only kind of soldier to be is the best there is. That's
why we went through all that infiltration hell. We've got to
be so good they'll never want to see us again.[15]

Our boys can really be tough when they must; and
they have to be tough because they have to do the
impossible.

Peter. The line between here and the Sened C.P. has been cut.
Can you get that patched up before lunch?

Simeon. There's no Jerries in there.

Peter. It must have been Arabs then, because the line's cut.
And the old man wants it in a hurry.

Simeon. The sappers haven't been through there yet! There's
mines all along the road and booby-traps at every pole. I'm
losing half my men already on those pioneer jobs.

Peter. You get out there and blow up those booby-traps and
miss those mines. And if you get yourself killed, I'll hold it
against you, because I need you for something else tonight.[16]

But they are not tough naturally; it's something they
have to learn.

Peter. He was killed because I made a mistake. And others were killed—because I made a mistake. I haven't learned how to be hard enough and ruthless enough. And I got them killed because of that. All right, I'll go ahead and learn to be ruthless and learn to be hard, and learn to be a better soldier, but I can't do it unless there's something beyond, unless there's something to come back to.[17]

Our nice boys overseas don't go chasing after harlots in their off moments. They get their mail from home and sit around showing one another pictures of their wives or girls.

We even have the "Praise the Lord and Pass the Ammunition" twaddle.

Sutton. Bring me the Book of Common Prayer and my pistols. This is getting to be a situation.

The problem of integrating the armies of the allied nations, one more item in the propaganda program, is at least shown to be a problem, and is rendered more interesting theatrically by the rivalry between the English and American officers over the nurse Tommy.

The story is buried almost out of sight under a profusion of army patter and local color. Except for the appearance of the necessary heroine, there is nothing in the first act but plans and reports, and a lot of good "clean dirt." The army lingo is so tidy, the effect of every oath and every bit of ribaldry so nicely calculated.

Still the Anderson touch is discernible in the not altogether incredible resolution of the magnificent complexity of Simeon's engineering exploits, and in the melodramatic marriage of Peter and Tommy during an air raid.

The couple has had a difficult time deciding to
marry. Again, as in *Key Largo*, the problem is the result
of a too close scrutiny of the values of life, produced in
this instance not by the sight of apparently needless
death, but of too much death. Mr. Anderson seems to
be groping for the truth that the only way to live life,
even in a time of mass disaster, is simply to live it. We
must go on with all the usual activities regardless of
hazards. If marriage is good, it is good without reference to the threat to its permanence. But the point
is too insistently urged. One hears the voice of the
author above the voices of his characters.

[1] Maxwell Anderson and Laurence Stallings, *What Price Glory*, in *Three
American Plays*, Harcourt, Brace and Company, New York, 1926, p. 3.
[2] Joseph Wood Krutch, *"Modernism"* in *Modern Drama*, Cornell University Press, Ithaca, New York, 1953, p. 109.
[3] ——, *The American Drama Since 1918*, Random House, New York,
1939, pp. 37-38.
[4] Maxwell Anderson and Harold Hickerson, *Gods of the Lightning*,
Longmans, Green and Company, New York, 1928, pp. 78-79.
[5] Maxwell Anderson, *Valley Forge*, in *Eleven Verse Plays*, Harcourt,
Brace and Company, New York, 1940, Act II, Scene II, pp. 115-116.
[6] *Ibid.*, Act I, Scene III, p. 62.
[7] *Ibid.*, Act II, Scene II, pp. 128-129.
[8] ——, *High Tor*, in *Eleven Verse Plays*, Act III, pp. 127-128.
[9] ——, *Key Largo*, in *Eleven Verse Plays*, Prologue, p. 23.
[10] *Ibid.*, Act II, p. 112.
[11] *Ibid.*, p. 114.
[12] *Ibid.*, pp. 117-118.
[13] ——, *Candle in the Wind*, Anderson House, Washington, D. C., 1941,
Act III, pp. 115-116.
[14] *Ibid.*, pp. 103-104.
[15] ——, *Storm Operation*, Anderson House, Washington, D. C., 1944,
Prologue, pp. 7-8.
[16] *Ibid.*, Act I, pp. 18-19.
[17] *Ibid.*, Act II, Scene III, p. 112.

CHAPTER VII

Romance

Maxwell Anderson got off to an auspicious start as a playwright with the chastening experience of failure with a play that was perhaps somewhat too arty, followed immediately by resounding success with one which took full account of the fact that a play must be "play" whatever else it is. With the possible exception of *Gods of the Lightning*, he never forgot the lesson. His next four plays after *What Price Glory* were entertainment first, and message, if any, only incidentally. Why *First Flight* and *The Buccaneer*, written by Anderson and Stallings, should have failed while *Outside Looking In* and *Saturday's Children* succeeded is not at all clear. All appear to the reader of thirty years after of approximately equal merit—or lack of merit. The explanation of Barrett H. Clark is probably the right one, that the audience expected from the collaboration of Stallings and Anderson another *What Price Glory*.

First Flight is hard to follow in reading, though it may have been less confusing to watch. There are too many unimportant characters. And the exposition of the political situation which brings the hero, the young Andrew Jackson, to the scene, is not well handled. It is too casual, too scattered, and hence too long delayed. And it is not worth so much trouble, because it is only an enveloping action for the romance.

The love story has real charm. There is an authentic folk quality, of the frontier variety, about the girl Charity. There is a simple dignity in the directness of the lovers. And there is a shimmering beauty cast over the final love duet by some rather nice poetry.

The Buccaneer is good melodrama of the musical comedy sort. The seventeenth-century English marauder Morgan, making a raid on Panama, runs into an English lady who is bored with the lack of excitement in Panama City. He is bold, bad, and irresistible to women. She is fearless, resourceful, and knows how to pique an irresistible man into being more irresistible. Together they create a series of ridiculous situations which give them opportunity to exhibit their powers. The third act takes them home to England, where the buccaneer and King Charles II discover that they are kindred spirits and join forces to circumvent British law and decorum for their own purposes and the delectation of the audience.

It is not difficult to account for the success of *Outside Looking In.* It is unabashed sentimentality. Yet the story gets on and has a certain interest and suspense. A couple of young innocents are fleeing from justice because the girl shot her beast of a stepfather, and they fall in with a nicely assorted collection of hoboes who have assembled to catch a train of empty freight cars going west. The more enterprising of the bums try to take the girl away from her devoted boy friend, Little Red, quarrel with one another over the right to do so, and of course quarrel with Little Red.

There is some difference of opinion as to whether these outcasts of society are or were intended to be authentic hoboes. Barrett H. Clark regards them as real tramps. But George Jean Nathan says, "Though the hoboes presented to us in the dramatization are diverting fellows, they smell less of actuality than of the vaudeville stage." I'm afraid I find their wit somewhat too sophisticated for reality, especially in the kangaroo court of the second act.

The burlesque of justice in the mock trial is far too clever and too obviously intended as satire to be successful social criticism. But it is an early example of Mr. Anderson's satiric method. More interesting because characteristic of his subtler ironic vein is the speech of Little Red which provokes the mock trial, a speech in which the author satirizes the very sentimentality toward the outcasts of society which he is exploiting in his story.

The last act is pure Bret Harte, with Oklahoma, the toughest of the hoboes, coming to the conclusion that "it must be love" and deciding to befriend the innocents. When word is brought that the sheriff with his posse is on their trail, Oklahoma orders the bums to stick together and give "the kids" a chance. He

hands over all his money to Little Red, tells them how
to get away, and holds his fellow tramps at bay while
the couple leaves. He is rewarded with a kiss and a
"good-bye, Old Timer," from the girl as she goes.

Nothing which Mr. Anderson has written belongs
more exclusively to the time for which it was produced
than his next play, *Saturday's Children*. To look at it
across the intervening years of depression and war and
the anxieties of the first atomic decade is to marvel
that the naïve irresponsibility with which the audience
is expected to sympathize could ever have seemed
touching or amusing. Not that the past quarter of a
century has made any change in the old tragi-comedy
of sex, for it has not. It was the brief period of the
twenties that gave the subject the peculiar little twist
which *Saturday's Children* has captured and preserved
as it could probably never be recaptured in retrospect.
It is one of the many literary embodiments of the idea
that marriage, particularly the financial aspect of the
partnership, is practically fatal to the love affair. The
novelty of *Saturday's Children* is that the children were
not representatives of sophisticated society, or disillu-
sioned victims of the First World War, or members of
the college smart set; nor were they poverty-stricken
waifs left over from the era of naturalism. Rims and
Bobby are a young couple of the workaday world who
don't know how to go on with their marriage after the
honeymoon is over. After a few quarrels over the management of their income Bobby walks out. She takes
a job again, lives in a rooming house, and once more
receives flowers and invitations to dinner.

Rims finds her out and calls on her. The rooming house is presided over by a suspicious matron who insists that girls must leave their doors open when entertaining gentlemen callers. Rims is obliged to leave, but returns later through the window with a bolt for the door. Then he and Bobby enjoy their clandestine love tryst. This is Bobby's idea of the real thing.

What they will do next is not revealed either by the reunited lovers or by their author. The disconcerting thing about the play is that the author, as well as the youngsters, seems to have believed at the time of his writing the play that the trouble was a too restricted income rather than too little understanding. Ignorance is often responsible for both comedy and tragedy. But ignorance must be recognized as the villain if either is to emerge. There is no recognition scene in *Saturday's Children*. The mistake remains unidentified.

Yet one can never dismiss an Anderson play as beneath consideration. There is too much of reality in even the least of them. The persons in this play are very much alive, not only the lovers, but also the kindly, sympathetic father, and Florrie, the sister. The problem, too, is a real one. Bobby is a sincere, straightforward person who despises tricks, but has no one to turn to for counsel except her sister. Florrie is a rather vicious specimen of the female schemer and parasite, who assures Bobby that husbands are always snared by ruses. Against her better feelings, Bobby acts on Florrie's advice to secure the proposal of marriage from Rims. But when the next crisis arises, after the marriage, and the sister is ready with the next trick, Bobby refuses to go on in this way. We are led to expect the resolution of this conflict, and we are disappointed when the play takes another turn and arrives nowhere.

We pass over five years to pick up the next romance, during which time Mr. Anderson wrote the realistic topical play *Gods of the Lightning* (with Harold Hickerson) and the eminently successful verse tragedy *Elizabeth the Queen.* The effect of these writing experiences as well as of the more serious mood of the thirties is evident in the more substantial character of *Night Over Taos.*

The romance here is in the struggle of an old and proud civilization to maintain its power and prestige unaltered against the inroads of new men and new ways. It is no hindrance to the enjoyment of the drama that the reader may not be well acquainted with the history of the conflict between the United States and Mexico in the 1840's. The pattern of the stories which arise out of such struggles is much the same whether they be of the French Revolution, the Scottish Highlanders, our own Civil War, or this conflict in the old Southwest.

Pablo Montoya is the autocratic ruler in Taos; his two sons, Federico and Felipe, the priest Martinez, and the Northern girl Diana represent the competing interests, desires, and convictions which precipitate the conflict. Martinez has a clear view of all the aspects of the situation.

Martinez. His father was lord of life and death before him, and he's been a god so long here in the valley that he thinks he's a god in fact. That's his strength, too, though it sometimes makes him a fool.[1]

The priest is expected to give advice, and does. He believes Taos could be saved by some small concessions. He has a printing press and has taught the peons to read. He would give them the franchise if they want it, knowing how much of form can be yielded without any power.

Montoya. And that's what you've meant
By your printing press ... and your teaching the peons to read!
Do you want a republic here?

Martinez. I want to save
What we have, Pablo. They're not all peons. They look
To the north and south, my friend, and take stock
   of themselves,
A little, and wonder why one class of men,
Or one man out of that class, has it all his own way
In the province of Taos.

Montoya. If so, it's because you've taught them
To think they can think.

Martinez. Not so. It came without asking,
Like an infection. There's only one cure for it,
And that's to seem to offer them from within
What's offered them outside. Give them books and schools,
And the franchise if they want it.

Montoya. You're my friend, José,
And have been, but this difference between us
Is deep as hell, and as wide. You fight the north
Because you want to keep your place. In your heart
You want what the north wants! But I fight the north
Because I despise what it stands for! Why should they think

About government, these peons? They're happier
With someone thinking for them! Why should the young
Take rank above their elders?

Martinez. We must give them the shadow
Or they'll want the substance.[2]

The crisis is brought about by an attack on Taos and
the belief that Don Pablo has been killed. If he is dead
Federico must then carry on. But Federico has betrayed
his father to the enemy in exchange for a guarantee of
half his father's estate. He is convinced that the Americans are the new men, that Taos is lost. He, like King
McCloud later, has no interest in dying for a lost cause.

Federico.   It's noble to die,
No doubt, when you have a noble cause to die for,
But when you have no cause, when your cause is lost,
The fewer lives lost the better.[3]

Felipe, the younger son, also sees the inevitability of
change, but he cannot deny his Spanish heritage. He is
his father's son. He will live or die by the code he has
received from his race. But he loves Diana, the young
girl whom Don Pablo intends to wed. He must not
confess his love. If he takes her in his arms, he will wish
his father dead. He does confess and take her in his arms.
He would save her. She is from the North. She need not
go down in the ruin of Taos. She tries to persuade him
that together they may seek freedom in the North, but he
belongs to Taos and is honor bound to stay.

When Don Pablo returns he quickly discovers
Federico's treachery and kills him in the sight of all the

people. Then he discovers Felipe's love for Diana and prepares to avenge that betrayal also. But suddenly, unaccountably, at the moment of dealing death to both of them, he withdraws his hand and drinks the poison himself, uttering such wisdom as would never have found its way through the mind and heart of such a man as Don Pablo. The ending is quite false. Still the play is a promise of better things soon to come. These slight romances constitute a kind of overture to the great romance of playwriting itself and represent the author's brief absorption in purely artistic considerations before his gifts were finally claimed by his dedication to the cause of freedom.

[1] Maxwell Anderson, *Night Over Taos*, in *Eleven Verse Plays*, Harcourt, Brace and Company, New York, 1940, Act I, p. 13.
[2] *Ibid.*, Act II, pp. 76-77.
[3] *Ibid.*, Act I, p. 49.

CHAPTER VIII

The Prophet
as Playwright

While the four plays now to be considered, *Winterset,
The Wingless Victory, High Tor,* and *The Star Wagon,*
make their comment, as do all Maxwell Anderson's
plays, on contemporary problems, their emphasis is on
character and universal values.

Mr. Anderson's undertaking to write verse tragedy
was a deliberate effort to recover something of supreme
value that had been lost. He observes in the essay
"Poetry in the Theatre" that writers sometimes make the
mistake of hoping the public is ready for a theme because they wish to treat it, or for a dramatic method
because they wish to employ it. Then he adds,

> I may have been somewhat guilty of this last misappre-
> hension in *Winterset,* for I have a strong and chronic hope
> that the theater of this country will outgrow the phase of
> journalistic social comment and reach occasionally into
> the upper air of poetic tragedy. I believe with Goethe
> that dramatic poetry is man's greatest achievement on
> his earth so far, and I believe with the early Bernard
> Shaw that the theater is essentially a cathedral of the
> spirit, devoted to the exaltation of men.[1]

Just what the nature of that exaltation is he defines more precisely in "The Uses of Poetry."

> ... the authors of tragedy offer the largest hope for mankind which I can discern in the great poetry of the earth, a hope that man is greater than his clay, that the spirit of man may rise superior to physical defeat and death. The theme of tragedy has always been victory in defeat, a man's conquest of himself in the face of annihilation. The last act of a tragedy contains the moment when the wheel of a man's fate carries him simultaneously to spiritual realization and to the end of his life. The message of tragedy is simply that men are better than they think they are, and this message needs to be said over and over again in every tongue lest the race lose faith in itself entirely.[2]

Why the poetic form is necessary to the exaltation he has also explained.

> To me it is inescapable that prose is the language of information and poetry the language of emotion. Prose can be stretched to carry emotion, and in some exceptional cases, as in Synge's and O'Casey's plays, can occasionally rise to poetic heights by substituting the unfamiliar speech rhythms of an untutored people for the rhythm of verse. But under the strain of an emotion the ordinary prose of our stage breaks down into inarticulateness, just as it does in life. Hence the cult of understatement, hence the realistic drama in which the climax is reached in an eloquent gesture or a moment of meaningful silence.[3]

We are not concerned, as Mr. Anderson was obliged to be, with whether the theatre public at any particular time may or may not be receptive to verse plays. Our

only concern, reading the play twenty years after its production, is whether *Winterset* is genuine poetic drama.

It is poetry, and it is tragedy; but it is not poetic
tragedy. Or rather, it is not dramatic poetry. The poetry
and the drama are not fused. The drama is very near to
greatness. The tragic effect is not so powerful as that of
Elizabeth the Queen, but the play is more original.

As with *Mary of Scotland,* one is struck with admiration at the rise of the curtain; for the scene is so evidently
more than mere setting. It is impressive in itself, and it
is rich with symbolic significance.

> The curtain rose on a stage of somber but breathtaking
> beauty. To the right the huge concrete pier of a bridge
> lifted itself sheer into the darkness above, and to the left
> a sullen block of tenements balanced the opposing mass.
> In the remote gloom of these lower depths the solid
> foundation of the proud bridge seemed a fitting monument
> to the dismal despair of the tenements, and the fact
> added meaning to the pure plastic beauty of the forms.
> Physically and spiritually the foundations upon which the
> city rests are seen from the perspective of those who
> crawl about their bases, and it is not often that the creative
> possibilities of stage design have been so convincingly
> demonstrated.[4]

The play presents the climax of a long search by the
young man Mio for evidence to clear the name of his
father, who was executed years ago for a crime he did
not commit. Public interest in the case has been rea-
wakened by some investigations of a professor revealing
that one of the witnesses, Garth Esdras, had not been
called. Mio has traced Garth Esdras to one of the tene-

ments of the scene just described. Trock Estrella, the real murderer, who has just been released from prison, appears at the same time, to insure Garth's silence. And finally, Judge Gaunt, who presided at the trial, is attracted to the spot. He is becoming mentally unbalanced under the strain of trying to convince himself that he did what was right. Maxwell Anderson's power to produce the effect of terror by exhibiting the tortured conscience is almost as great as Hawthorne's. Again Krutch pronounces the Anderson method classical rather than revolutionary.

> Obviously there is in all this no lack of exciting action or of opportunity for direct socio-political argument. But both are subordinated as they would be in a classic tragedy to a brooding and poetic treatment of the themes which the action suggests—namely, the nature of guilt and of justice and the meaning of revenge.[5]

When the opportunity for revenge, or for vindicating his father presents itself—it is part of Mio's tragedy that he confuses the two—when all who have injured him, the real murderer, the corrupt judge, and the long-silent witness are delivered into his hands, he is unable to go through with his purpose. For he has fallen in love with the sister of Garth Esdras. "I've lost my taste for revenge if it falls on you," he tells her. Her love redeems him from the bitterness and hate which have for so long been his daily companions. But, with true classic irony, his bitterness has already laid a snare which is to trip him just as he emerges from the shadow of despair. When a police officer, in the routine discharge of his duty, breaks up the dancing in the street, Mio baits him, ridicules him. Later, when the same officer comes to the Esdras apartment when Mio has Trock at bay, charging him with murder, Mio tells the policeman he will find the "corpse" in the next room, but the officer thinks he is being badgered again and refuses to be duped. The moment passes. Trock is allowed to get away, and Mio's life is then in peril.

He has no desire to escape. He has lost his thirst for vengeance, but he has not found a hope. He remains talking with Miriamne while Trock and his henchmen cut off his retreat. His friend Carr returns and speaks with him briefly, but Mio lets him go without asking for help. Then, when it is too late, hope dawns, and he wishes to live. He tries to escape and is shot. In a frenzy of grief Miriamne cries out to the killers that she knows all Mio knew and will tell. And she too is shot.

Most readers are offended by the lamentation and prophecy of old Esdras—the "Pseudo-rabbinical peroration," John Gassner calls it—with which the play ends. But this speech is at worst merely extraneous. It is not to be taken as a statement of the theme of the play. It is such a comment as Esdras might be expected to make. The true illumination is that which comes to Mio when the chains which have bound him fall away.

Mio. Miriamne, if you love me
teach me a treason to what I am, and have been,
till I learn to live like a man! I think I'm waking
from a long trauma of hate and fear and death
that's hemmed me from my birth—and glimpse a life
to be lived in hope—but it's young in me yet, I can't

get free, or forgive! But teach me how to live
and forget to hate!

Miriamne. He would have forgiven.

Mio. He?

Miriamne. Your father.

Mio. Yes.
You'll think it strange, but I've never
remembered that.

Miriamne. How can I help you?

Mio. You have.

Miriamne. If I were a little older—if I knew
the things to say! I can only put out my hands
and give you back the faith you bring to me
by being what you are. Because to me
you are all hope and beauty and brightness drawn
across what's black and mean!

Mio. He'd have forgiven—
Then there's no more to say—I've groped long enough
through this everglades of old revenges—here
the road ends.—Miriamne, Miriamne,
the iron I wore so long—it's eaten through
and fallen from me. Let me have your arms.
They'll say we're children—Well—the world's made up
of children.

Miriamne. Yes.

Mio. But it's too late for me.

Miriamne. No.

(*She goes into his arms, and they kiss for the first time*)

Then we'll meet again?

Mio. Yes.

Miriamne. Where?

Mio. I'll write—
or send Carr to you.

Miriamne. You won't forget?

Mio. Forget?
Whatever streets I walk, you'll walk them, too,
from now on, and whatever roof or stars
I have to house me, you shall share my roof
and stars and morning. I shall not forget.

Miriamne. God keep you!

Mio. And keep you. And this to remember!
if I should die, Miriamne, this half-hour
is our eternity. I came here seeking
light in darkness, running from the dawn,
and stumbled on a morning.[6]

It has been observed that Maxwell Anderson often
seems to be saying more than he actually says. I have
felt this to be true many times, felt it with something
like exasperation. This passage, for instance:

I came here seeking

light in darkness, running from the dawn,
and stumbled on a morning.

Does it make any sense? How was he running from the
dawn? Running from the darkness—that he was doing.
How are dawn and morning to be opposed?

Dawn is the word we use for the promise of morning.
It is the symbol of an ideal, absolute truth, the perfect
justice Mio was seeking. He was running from it, driven
by the hate and bitterness which made him unfit to be an
instrument for righting the wrong which had been done.

As a promise dawn is also an incomplete thing. It is
not the full light of day. Justice is not the whole truth,
the whole good. Running from the uncertain struggle
between darkness and dawn, between despair and desire
of good, he stumbles upon love, upon the full light of
morning. Morning is the light of common day, not a
theoretical absolute good, but the light which shines
alike upon the evil and the good and conquers darkness
by displacing it.

Whether all of Mr. Anderson's metaphors would yield
so rich a meaning on closer scrutiny I cannot say. But I
am warned once more against a hasty dismissal of anything which he writes. It is not, however, through an
examination of the imagery that we can determine
whether or not the verse is dramatic poetry.

The first objection, which the passage just quoted
illustrates, is that the blank verse scans but it does not
throb. It lacks the strong movement of the eloquence of
passion. It is reflective. As a statement of the resolution
of the conflict it is dramatic, for it expresses the hero's
discovery of something "of which he has not been aware

—or which he has not taken sufficiently into account."
And that discovery will mean a complete change in his
course of action. The outcome answers exactly to the
definition of tragedy already cited in this chapter.

> The theme of tragedy has always been victory in defeat,
> a man's conquest of himself in the face of annihilation.
> The last act of tragedy contains the moment when the
> wheel of a man's fate carries him simultaneously to spirit-
> ual realization and to the end of his life.[7]

But as a climax of the play the verse lacks the necessary
excitement. Mio's self-realization does not come with the
impact of immediate discovery. Despite the lift in the
language, the syntax and the phrasing are prose.

In other passages the poetry fails as dramatic poetry
for another and more subtle reason. It is not dramatic
because it does not express the thoughts and feelings
of the persons who speak it. I do not mean by this that
the expression ought to be realistic. I mean that it is
something quite different from that heightened awareness as well as heightened expression which is permitted
to the characters in poetic drama. It is symbolic poetry.
What we hear in the following lines is not the voice of
the author conveying in absolute symbols a mature vision
of young love and a mature compassion for its predicament.

Mio. So now little Miriamne will go in
and take up quietly where she dropped them all
her small housewifely cares.—When I first saw you,
not a half-hour ago, I heard myself saying,
this is the face that launches ships for me—

and if I owned a dream—yes, half a dream—
we'd share it. But I have no dream. This earth
came tumbling down from chaos, fire and rock,
and bred up worms, blind worms that sting each other
here in the dark. These blind worms of the earth
took out my father—and killed him, and set a sign
on me—the heir of the serpent—and he was a man
such as men might be if the gods were men—
but they killed him—
as they'll kill all others like him
till the sun cools down to the stabler molecules,
yes, till men spin their tent-worm webs to the stars
and what they think is done, even in the thinking,
and they are the gods, and immortal, and constellations
turn for them all like mill wheels—still as they are
they will be worms and blind. Enduring love,
oh gods and worms, what mockery!—And yet
I have blood enough in my veins. It goes like music,
singing, because you're here. My body turns
as if you were the sun, and warm. This men called love
in happier times, before the Freudians taught us
to blame it on the glands. Only go in
before you breathe too much of my atmosphere
and catch death from me.

Miriamne. I will take my hands
and weave them to a little house, and there
you shall keep a dream—

Mio. God knows I could use a dream
and even a house.

Miriamne. You're laughing at me, Mio!

Mio. The worms are laughing.

* * *

Mio. Why, girl, the transfiguration on the mount
was nothing to your face. It lights from within—
a white chalice holding fire, a flower in flame,
this is your face.

Miriamne. And you shall drink the flame
and never lessen it. And round your head
the aureole shall burn that burns there now,
forever. This I can give you. And so forever
the Freudians are wrong.[8]

These are not the words of a boy and girl in the rap-
ture of first love. The lines are pure symbols, represent-
ing, not expressing, the music of the emotions. The
failure of the poetry is due not only to the fact that the
breadth of knowledge is incredible from a realistic point
of view, but also and chiefly to the sophisticated use of
that knowledge. The point of view is detached. It is
young love perceived, not experienced.

There is one further objection to the poetry. The
poetic flights are flights. They break away from their
context. They are not like the arias in grand opera, which,
though identifiable as set pieces, do not attract undue
attention to themselves because they are in a musical
context. The verse of the realistic base of the play is so
close to prose that passages like the one just quoted
cannot fail to seem artificial. Yet when all objections are
registered, when the probing is over, the play regains its
dignity, reasserts its validity.

The Wingless Victory is a romantic tragedy which
would be great if the hero were worthy of tragic treatment. Nathaniel McQueston is an adventurer in the days

of the Salem clipper ships. He ran away to sea when he was young. He amassed a fortune, fell in love with a Malayan princess, stole a ship, stole the princess, and made off for home. And why for home, knowing what kind of home he had left? To show off. To flaunt his riches, and torment his pious Puritan family by bringing a dark-skinned wife into their smug little New England town.

He finds his family in a gratifying state of financial collapse, unable to reject him because he comes with money. He exults in his power over them. But since he acquired his wealth by piracy, he has no understanding of the management of money and falls an easy prey to the shrewd New Englanders on whom he has declared social warfare.

His motives are little better than those of the Salem people he flouts. He has a kind of impulsive generosity and affection, and the love of a woman who is his superior in every respect calls out the best that is in him. But he has no depth, no roots. He is as dependent on money and its prestige as the Puritans he despises, and dependent, too, on their acceptance of him. He will have their approval by force, as he has his wealth. But he must have both. When he is outmaneuvered by his brother he collapses at once, denying even his love. He has no resources of knowledge or wisdom or fortitude for making a place for himself and his wife in any other spot on the earth. We are made to feel his suffering, his helplessness in the isolation he cannot face. But he is merely pathetic, not tragic.

Oparre is magnificent. She is one of Mr. Anderson's

greatest creations. Her courtesy is like the incense of her
perfume in the bleak New England house. Her passion is
a bright flame. The poetry she speaks is beautiful with
the strange beauty of her own exotic nature.

Of the play as a whole, the unity of tone is damaged
by a greater emphasis on race tensions than the romance
requires. Oparre's denunciation of the white race, and of
Christianity as inseparable from that race, is so all-
inclusive and expressed in such general terms that it
is impossible not to suppose that social criticism is
intended.

Oparre. Come in!
All these white frightened faces, come in and hear!
We have news for you. I have been misled
a long time by your Christ and his beggar's doctrine,
written for beggars! Your beseeching, pitiful Christ!
The old gods are best, the gods of blood and bronze,
and the arrows dipped in venom! You worship them, too,
Moloch and Javeh of your Old Testament,
requiring sacrifice of blood, revenging
all save their chosen! You vouchsafe no pity
to the alien, and I'll give none. I have been a princess,
and I remember that gladly now. I come
of a race that can go mad and strike! Why, yes,
you fear me, and you should! Your pallid lips
and pallid hands and hearts, your milky hearts
that know neither love nor hate, your weasel warren
that squeaks and clusters! What could there be between us,
between the eagle and the rat, save death—?[9]

Oparre. Why was this body gathered out of dust
and bitten to my image? Let that day be evil
when a lover took a lover to mould the face

that stares up blind from my agony! Stares up
and cries, and will not be still! Let all women born
take a man's love with laughter, and leave it; take
the coil of animals they give, and rise
in mockery. And you dark peoples of the earth,
cling to your dark, lie down and feed and sleep
till you are earth again; but if you love,
love only children of the dark—keep back
from the bright hair and white hands, for they are light
and cruel, like the gods', and the love that breeds
between us is honeyed poison. Let no flesh
of theirs touch flesh of yours; where they have touched
the welt rots inward! They are unclean, unclean
and leprous to us! To lie with them is sweet,
but sweet with death! I bear that death in me
in a burning tide that rises—choking—Oh, God—
torture me no more![10]

As dramatic expression these lines are superb, and if
Nathaniel were more nearly a match for Oparre it would
not be necessary to regard them as anything other than
dramatic. As social criticism the cards are stacked against
the West. Oparre is made the bearer of the most enlightened view of the twentieth century and is pitted against
a pirate and a few seventeenth-century Puritans as
representatives of the white race and of Christianity.
Nothing new is done with the Puritans. They are stock
figures. Everything is done with Oparre.

Some dozen years later Mr. Anderson found a more
suitable vehicle for his ideas on race relations in the
novel *Cry, the Beloved Country* by Alan Paton; and
Lost in the Stars is a better play than *The Wingless
Victory* because in it the artist and social commentator

are at one, the drama completely embodies the theme.

The same observation can be made in regard to *Winterset* as compared with *Gods of the Lightning*. As an attempt to dramatize miscarriage of justice, *Gods of the Lightning* fails because social criticism predominates over theatre.

Yet it is not even in *Winterset*, good as it is, that Mr. Anderson's hope for the triumph of art over journalistic comment is most fully realized. For that victory we must turn to the comedies, *High Tor* and *The Star Wagon*.

In *High Tor* Mr. Anderson's imagination kicked over the traces and took off untrammeled to "paw up against light, and do strange deeds/Upon the clouds." It is such fantasy as might justify the genre almost unaided. Mr. Anderson has given a new meaning to the word "play," or revived the one it had when it meant *A Midsummer Night's Dream* and *The Tempest*. How so penetrating a critic as Joseph Wood Krutch could define fantasy as "only imagination not powerful enough to convince itself" is incredible when we have *High Tor* to gainsay the definition. In fantasy the poet, in his fine frenzy, reverses the usual process, and gives to local somethings an airy habitation and a name. The method is that described by Kenneth Burke in his essay "Lexicon Rhetorica": the content embodies the form. The order, the completeness, is in the spiritual realm, with the actual world breaking through somewhat incongruously, as in ordinary experience mystical appearances seem to be an interruption of the established order.

It is impossible to make a résumé of the action of

High Tor, for the detail is everything and there are three long acts of detail. Yet Mr. Anderson's control over his volatile material is as firm as if it were a set of well-known historical facts. His ingenuity in fabricating an intricate plot is nowhere more freely but surely operative. The thing is a bubble, but is made of nylon.

The scene is a small mountain on the upper Hudson. A real estate firm wishes to level the mountain to build a resort; but the owner, Van Van Dorn, refuses to sell. He represents the natural man, the last of the breed, resisting the mechanistic age. The incidents through which the conflict is developed are riotously amusing. But the play, in addition to being hilarious entertainment, is a sharp satire on materialistic values. I think it is a mistake to look for the meaning of the play in any of the single lines which have so much the appearance of theme statements.

Van.   Maybe I'm ghost myself
trying to hold an age back with my hands. (Act II, Scene II.)

The Indian. ... there's no hill worth a man's peace
while he may live and find it. (Act III.)

The Indian.   Nothing is made by men
but makes, in the end, good ruins. (Act III.)

Nothing in the way of a literal meaning or a solution is to be assumed from Van's conclusion:

Van. I guess if you were with me then we'd sell
for what we could, and move out farther west
where a man's land's his own. (Act II, Scene II.)

The meaning of play is in the whole construct, in the imaginative discernment of the past within the present, in the removal of the wall between the material and the spiritual, in the juxtaposition and constant interplay of the ideal and the actual.

The bewitched figures, the survivors of the Dutch ship, desire to be real, to survive; but when the mountain is gone they will be gone.

Asher. You have seen us in the sun,
wraithlike, half-effaced, the print we make
upon the air thin tracery, permeable,
a web of wind. They have changed us. We may take
the fire-balls of the lightning in our hands
and bowl them down the level floor of cloud
to wreck the beacon, yet there was a time
when these were death to touch. The life we keep
is motionless as the center of a storm,
yet while we can we keep it; while we can
snuff out to darkness their bright sweeping light,
melt down the harness of the slow machines
that hew the mountain from us. When it goes
we shall go too.[11]

When the forms of the past are gone, the past is dead. Is that what the play seems to say? Lise wonders if they may not stay alive by falling in love with the new creatures. We are reminded of one of the proverbs in Blake's *Marriage of Heaven and Hell*: "Eternity is in love with the productions of time." Only if the present loves the past will it keep that past alive. What has power to live, to continue? When Judith comes looking for Van she finds him sleeping with his head in the lap of the past. But Lise assures her, "He'll wake, and he'll be yours." And it is true.

The verse in this play is decidedly superior to that of *Winterset*. The lines spoken by Asher quoted above are a good example. They do not try to make up in forced imagery for metrical and syntactical deficiencies. These lines move with the nervous energy of authentic blank verse.

So brief a comment seems a disproportionate treatment of one of the few unequivocally great of Maxwell Anderson's plays. I have given no idea of the wonderful incongruities which result from allowing a couple of hardheaded emissaries of the commercial interests to be stranded on the mountain top with the ghosts of Henry Hudson's crew and forcing them to spend the night in the bucket of their own idle steam shovel; but I cannot bring myself to violate the delicate balance of the whole exquisite fabrication by quoting fragments. I have made special mention of the time concept in this play, because it is a recurring theme in the plays of Maxwell Anderson and is the whole substance of that other fantasy, *The Star Wagon*. But the reader is not to expect that the play is a set of precise symbols. It is a free fantasy with no better object and no greater merit than its sheer fun.

The Star Wagon is also fantasy, but is not so successful as *High Tor*. There are some loose ends in its construction. The exposition in the opening scene is bald. The dream of the herb woman (Act II, Scene IV),

which is obviously intended to make an important comment, contributes nothing except some philosophical
vagaries. The use of a few lines from Dryden for making
the connection between the scene of the false future
(Act II, Scene I) and the final scene is inept. Dryden is
scarcely the poet to be remembered casually by such a
person as Martha or to be familiar to the average theatre-
goer. Mr. Anderson's use of literary allusion is frequently
more academic than theatrical.

Yet these are trifling defects. The play is good entertainment. The leading character is a type Mr. Anderson
loves: the impractical dreamer, quaint, humorous,
slightly pestiferous, so egotistical as to be quite incapable of understanding the wife who cannot share his
absorbing pursuit but must bear the brunt of its depri-
vations. Stephen Minch, an inventor, is a more credible
and a more attractive specimen than Socrates. Of course
he has the advantage of a happy ending, inventions being
of greater value to a democracy than ideas! The satire on
materialism is the more effective in these fantasies than
in other plays for being free of any rancor.

Stephen has invented a machine by which any time
out of the past can be tuned in as any place may be
tuned in on a radio. It is used to transport the characters
to their youth for the purpose of rectifying their wrong
choices. They return in the last scene, chastened by their
vision of what might have been, to an acceptance of the
road they took as after all the right one.

The most amusing episode is the scene (Act I,
Scene III) in which the inventor employs a couple of

ordinary thugs to help him steal his time machine from the laboratory of the company from which he has just been fired. The delightful absurdities which develop out of their cross-purposes and failures to communicate are in Mr. Anderson's best vein of humor.

High Tor and *The Star Wagon* were written when Mr. Anderson was at his creative best, when he was most free in the exercise of his imaginative powers. And fantasy gives full scope to that wonderful gift of playfulness —the exercise of the faculties of thought and feeling for the sheer delight of their play—which is one of his most engaging traits. Unfortunately the remembrance of Caliban blasted the "visionary splendor" at the moment of its exhilarating triumph. In the preface to *Journey to Jerusalem* Mr. Anderson says that faith is the only answer to Hitler, to the materialism and philosophy of "might makes right" which Hitler epitomized. Doubtless faith must come first. But the humor, the ironic but entirely good-natured humor of the fantasies, must be an almost equally indispensable antidote. It is to be hoped that Maxwell Anderson will find a moment of leisure from the anxieties of the atomic age to try once more as a corrective for the despair of our time his healing gift of laughter.

[1] Maxwell Anderson, *Off Broadway*, William Sloane Associates, Inc., New York, 1947, p. 48.

[2] *Ibid.*, p. 90.

[3] *Ibid.*, p. 50.

[4] Joseph Wood Krutch, *The American Drama Since 1918*, Random House, New York, 1939, p. 295.

[5] *Ibid.*, p. 297.

[6] Maxwell Anderson, *Winterset*, in *Eleven Verse Plays*, Harcourt, Brace and Company, New York, 1940, Act III, pp. 125-127.

[7] ———, *Off Broadway*, p. 90.

[8] ———, *Winterset*, in *Eleven Verse Plays*, Act I, Scene III, pp. 47-49.

[9] ———, *The Wingless Victory*, in *Eleven Verse Plays*, Act II, p. 109.

[10] *Ibid.*, Act III, Scene I, p. 117.

[11] ———, *High Tor*, in *Eleven Verse Plays*, Act I, Scene II, pp. 31-32.

CHAPTER IX

Jesus and Joan,
the Final Affirmation

In his essay "The Essence of Tragedy" Maxwell Anderson observes that men for fifty generations have been seeking, without entire success, to define tragedy and to explain to themselves its appeal and its effect. He has not solved the riddle, but he is willing to make his contribution to the united effort.

Speaking from the point of view of the writer he defines tragedy in terms of the hero, and his definition is simple: "He must learn through suffering." Obviously this definition requires some elaborating, and Mr. Anderson provides the elaboration.

The mainspring of a play is a discovery by the hero of something in himself or his environment of which he has not been aware, a discovery "which has an indelible effect on his thought and emotion and completely alters his course of action." The alteration must be a change for the better.

153

In other words, a hero must pass through an experience which opens his eyes to an error of his own. He must learn through suffering. In a tragedy he suffers death itself as a consequence of his fault or his attempt to correct it, but before he dies he has become a nobler person because of his recognition of his fault and the consequent alteration of his course of action. In a serious play which does not end in death he suffers a lesser punishment, but the pattern remains the same. In both forms he has fault to begin with, he discovers that fault during the course of the action, and he does what he can to rectify it at the end.... From the point of view of the playwright, then, the essence of a tragedy, or even of a serious play, is the spiritual awakening, or regeneration, of his hero.[1]

Mr. Anderson's *Journey to Jerusalem* is an almost academic translation of this definition into a hero and his discovery of an error in himself. It is the story of the boy Jesus, who, at the age of twelve, made the trip with his parents to the temple at Jerusalem for the celebration of the Passover. While he is there he becomes convinced that he is the expected Messiah. He had thought it might be so—he had had a dream; but he was not sure. He is perplexed by the anxiety of his parents, by their caution and that of the prophet Ishmael. Why is everyone so uneasy? Is it not a glorious hope? The Messiah is to win victories; in his dream he has seen himself at the head of a victorious host. Through Ishmael he learns of his error. The Messiah is not to triumph over his enemies. He is to suffer and to die. And Jesus sees Ishmael die on the spot for telling him this truth. It is a shock; but he rises from the side of the dead prophet to face unflinching the soldiers of Herod.

The play is not dramatic. There is no struggle, no conflict. It is a little allegory of the author's definition of tragedy: man is made perfect through suffering. As such it was probably valuable to the playwright himself as preparation for his great drama of faith, *Joan of Lorraine.*

In *Joan of Lorraine* Mr. Anderson asks what he considers to be the ultimate question: "Why do you believe what you believe?" And now to look back over the way which he has come is to see that it has been a straight and narrow way leading inevitably to this story of martyrdom. Ever since he asked his first question "What price glory?" he has gone on asking his questions and seeking the answers. Even in the simple romances of the twenties he was asking his questions. In *Saturday's Children* he asked by what authority lovers are kept apart before they are married and forced together afterwards. In many plays he asked the question, What price justice? In many, What price freedom? In many, What price love? And now at last, What price faith? And everywhere the answer has been the same: You must die for what you believe to be right because the only alternative is to embrace what you know to be wrong.

Men have perceived this truth in war; but war is just another evasion of personal responsibility. A military organization is another authority, like the medieval church, which violates the individual conscience. It is a long way from war to personal martyrdom, and that is the way which Mr. Anderson has explored in the whole course of his art. Even in war men die alone. There is no escaping the individual choice. And so the old story of

the Maid of Orleans is the right story for the dramatization of the ultimate question, What price integrity?

Again Mr. Anderson's artistic intuition is operating
with that full, free, unfrightened abandon which we
have noted all along. It does not matter that a play
within a play is no invention of his own. It is the device
he needs for his purpose and that is enough. He is as free
as Shakespeare of any petty vanity about receiving from
others. He uses old things as fearlessly as new, but always
he makes something new of them.

The play within a play enables the author to con-
front his contemporaries with the same question which
Joan faced. Shall the actors do a play which does not
say what they want to say? Shall the director cover a
bad check for the man who is to provide them with a
theatre? These are representative questions, bringing
the ultimate question of martyrdom out of the dim
light of the cathedral, out of the dim past of the fifteenth
century, into the place where it matters most, where
men do the work by which they live. War is artificial.
In the temporary relapse in which Mr. Anderson tried
to revive its glory his hero—Private Quizz West of *The
Eve of St. Mark* (Act II, Scene IV)—comes in a vision
to ask his mother, shall he come home or stay and hold
the island? His mother answers, "It's better to live. If
you live now you can fight them again." Why live to
fight them again? Would he not fight for the same
things again? And if he would, why not fight it out now?
Joan of Lorraine presents the truer insight. It is not
only in war that we face the ultimate question. We are
forced to face it in war only because we refuse to face

it day by day. War is only the terrific explosion built up by a million daily evasions. Mr. Anderson's hero and heroine face the question in the midst of a day's work.

And what is their answer?

It seems best to follow the course by which they arrive at their answer; for that is the drama.

The dramatic situation is a play rehearsal in which the actors and director try to explain to themselves the meaning of the drama they are producing. It is the story of Joan of Arc; and the director, Jimmy Masters, and the leading actress, Mary Gray, have almost come to a parting of the ways over the interpretation. They plan to have lunch together to quarrel about it. But before the lunch hour arrives it turns out that the other members of the cast are also interested in the question.

Masters. . . . When Joan was nineteen years old, after she'd crowned her king and saved France, she was captured by her enemies and put on trial for her life. And they asked her the toughest question ever put to the human race. Why do you believe what you believe? Remember that? It's in the second act.

Noble. "Why do you believe what you believe?"

Masters. That's right. That's the question we all have to answer. And that's the big scene in anybody's life, when he has to answer that question.[2]

They go forward with the rehearsal, and through the directions to the players Mr. Anderson justifies his use of the story which so many writers have already used. He does not like the portrait which represents Joan as mannish. His play is a reinterpretation. He believes she was completely feminine, but imitated her brother's manner as the only way which she could find for speaking to rulers and soldiers. And he weaves this concept into the structure of the play. Joan's apparent insincerity is later to become a stumbling block for her, but at the moment she sees it in its true light.

Joan. . . . God help me, it's a kind of play-acting, a thing forbidden, yet if it's the only way it must be God's way.

In the course of the morning Masters finds that he will have to cancel his luncheon engagement with Mary in order to see someone about a theatre. He explains the matter to her in one of the interludes between scenes.

Masters. My dear Mary, you haven't had much experience with theatre business in New York. It's frightening. You find yourself dealing with all sorts of shady operators. You heard me saying that the theatre we're supposed to open in turns out to be rented from a man who put through a minor swindle to get the lease on it—and he's in jail, and if we don't cover a bad check of his he'll stay there and lose his lease and we can't open.[3]

It is just this matter of compromise which is troubling Mary. The play is being rewritten with a new meaning which she is not willing to countenance. Since they can't lunch together, they try to settle the question before he goes out. In fact, they merely continue an argument that has been going on all along.

Mary. But it seems to me the way the play is now it means that we all have to compromise and work with evil men—and that if you have a faith it will come to nothing unless you get some of the forces of evil on your side.

Masters. That's right. I don't think I'd call them the forces of evil—but you have to get some of the people who are running things on your side—and they're pretty doubtful characters mostly.

Mary. But is that what we want to say, in a play about Joan of Arc?[4]

Mary is disappointed.

Mary. . . . I have always wanted to play Joan. I have studied her and read about her all my life. She has a meaning for me. She means that the great things in this world are all brought about by faith—that all the leaders who count are dreamers and people who see visions. The realists and the common-sense people can never begin anything. They can only do what the visionaries plan for them. The scientists can never lead unless they happen to be dreamers, too.[5]

Masters agrees.
Then how can he defend compromise?
His defense is not very impressive. What Dunois says later is much better.

Act II takes place on the rehearsal stage an hour later. Masters is back from lunch; and while they wait for Mary the actors begin asking Masters questions. Why not live by common sense? Why not live by science? Masters answers that neither of these tell you what direction to take. The others protest that they have no faith.

Masters. Oh, yes, you do. And you live by it. Everybody has a notion of what the world's like and what he's like in it. . . . A man has to have a faith, and a culture has to have one—

Finally someone asks Masters what his religion is.

Masters. I guess democracy. I believe in democracy, and I believe the theatre is the temple of democracy. A democratic society needs a church without a creed—where anybody is allowed to talk as long as he can hold an audience—and that's what the theatre is—though it's sort of dwindling down to a side-chapel here, lately.[6]

This is Mr. Anderson's own faith, as he has expressed it in many places, but particularly in the essay "Thoughts about the Critics."

> Personally I don't trust any critic—or anybody else, including myself—to know when a play has said something worth listening to or worth saving. I do trust the public in a democracy. That's the only faith I have.[7]

To return to the play, when the actors resume their rehearsal they are doing the scene at the Rheims Cathedral. Dunois tells the Dauphin that the military leaders have decided to march at once on Paris. But the Dauphin in consideration of a good round sum, has just sent Tremoille to accept Burgundy's plea for a two-week truce. So he tells them they may not march on Paris. They protest, and he defies them. Joan insisted on making him king; and if he is to be king he is going to rule.

Dauphin. What do you three know of the expedients to which the heads of nations must stoop? What do you know of statecraft? You are children in such matters. A ruler has to rob, murder, compromise, lie, cheat, steal, and enter into compacts with all sorts of brigands in order to keep going!—

Joan. But you did all these things before I came—and they didn't help!

Dauphin. And do you think your coming has reformed the methods of government? Men have been governed by corruption since the invention of government. They like it. They don't want to be governed any other way! And if you think a green girl from the country is going to change that by winning some victories you have more delusions than I thought.

Joan. Men hate corruption! And God hates it!

Dauphin. I don't know about God, but men take to it very naturally. You promised me I'd have money when I needed it, remember? Well, I need it very badly, and God does nothing about it.

Joan. And now I begin to wonder why God wished you to be King.

Dauphin. I wondered that myself when you first came to me, but you explained it very convincingly at the time. And now that I'm to be made King, and practically am King, I tell you I shall do as I please. And I please to make a truce with Burgundy, and maybe I shall never march on Paris at all. Maybe I'll decide that it's wiser not to.[8]

Dunois has the simple, direct way of a soldier, even to his faith. It is he who holds Joan to her vision when she wavers. And his justification of the apparent compromise is better than that of Masters in the earlier passage.

Dunois. Don't leave him. Stay with him.

Joan. After he has betrayed us all—and his country—and even himself?

Dunois. Yes. You see, if you speak out you may destroy him, and if you do that you'll destroy all you've accomplished—for France will have no king. And if you speak out and he's crowned anyway, and you leave him, what will France have? A government of pure corruption. No saint, no faith, no good angel, no good influence—just corruption. But if you stay with him he will have to think a little of the people of France, and not always of his own bargains, for the people of France will trust you, and he will sometimes have to listen to you.

Joan. But would I be honest to stay—to stand here at his crowning and say nothing about what he has done?

Dunois. Didn't your Voices tell you that you were to set the Dauphin on the throne in the cathedral at Rheims?

Joan. Yes.

Dunois. Well—this is the Dauphin—the only one we have—and this is the cathedral—and the doors are about to be opened. You are doing what God told you to do.

La Hire. It makes a man wonder if God would be wrong.

Joan. No. He could not be wrong. This is the king. He chose and He could not be wrong. And yet—

Dunois. Every Government is made up of bargainers, Joan. That's to be expected. Even God must be aware of that. And it's a lucky country where the bargainers don't have it all their own way—where there's somebody like you about, making the bargainers behave.[9]

This is the part which Mary objects to.

Mary. All the rest I can believe—but I don't see how she can decide so deliberately to give her blessing to corruption.

It appears that even the author cannot understand this, judging from his labored efforts to justify it. But the fact is Joan was not compromising; she was simply obeying the voice of God.

The next scene is the trial. Cauchon, the Bishop of Beauvais, states the case as he sees it. He is the voice of expediency. Joan must be discredited. But the Inquisitor will not be swayed by secular interests or by any considerations of policy. He proceeds with great care.

Inquisitor. Here is the case against you. You hear voices, have visions and inspirations, which you say come from God. The church, which is God's representative on earth, does not recognize the possibility of direct inspiration from God to His children. If you have visions we must condemn them as evil and condemn you as evil. Unless—unless—you see, there is a way out—unless you also condemn your visions as evil.

Joan. But I know that my Voices are good.

Inquisitor. How do you know it?

Joan. I am sure of it. I know them well.

Inquisitor. You see, you have no proof. It is impossible for you to have proof.

Joan. What they led me to do was good.

Inquisitor. Can you be sure that it was good? Think of your king, and the men around him. Can you be sure? Be truthful.

Joan. No. I am not sure.

Inquisitor. At last! She has said it!

Joan. Oh, can't you see that what I want is to do right, and not
to do wrong? Can't you see that this is my greater torture? More
than the torment of the guards, more than the torment of the lack
of sleep, more than the threat of the fire—this torment of not
knowing whether I am right or wrong? My Voices came to me
when I was a child, and I loved them and worshipped them, and
I have followed them all my life. But don't you see that I would
give them up instantly if I knew they were evil? Only I don't
know. And you haven't told me. What is all this trial for? I wish
to do right. It's because I wish to do right that I stand out
stubbornly through these sleepless nights and try to find God's
way in my thinking!

Inquisitor. Yes, you are saved, Joan! We shall beat the fire yet!

Joan. But I will not be trapped! I will not betray the truth to
avoid the fire!

Inquisitor. Never! I would as soon betray myself! But the way is
easy and clear now. You have come to the great question—the one
that goes to the root—the one to which all thinking men must
come—why do I believe what I believe? Isn't that it?

Joan. Yes. Then you do know.

Inquisitor. I came to it myself, though not so young as you. I
came to it in middle age, and it tortured me as it tortures you
now. And I fought my way through to an answer. Do you wish
to know what it was?

Joan. With all my heart.

Inquisitor. It is this! One must believe nothing which cannot be

solidly proved. All hopes, all dreams, all aspirations, all ima-
ginings, must be ruthlessly emptied out. The soul must be rinsed
to the bottom of all these things—and must hold only to what
can be proved.

Joan. But then what is there that can be proved?

Inquisitor. The doctrine and the teachings of the church. They
come down in unbroken succession from the word of God.
Nothing else is solid. Nothing else can be proved.[10]

Joan knows she can prove nothing. She is persuaded to renounce her visions and submit to the Church.
But this is not the end.

Joan's prayer in the prison is one of the most truly
beautiful passages in all of Mr. Anderson's writing; and
it is not poetry but prose. He had said that great utterances require poetry, but he is not betrayed by a "fool-
ish consistency." His taste is true as it was true when he
employed the most conventional form in *Elizabeth the
Queen* to reveal by contrast the originality of his new
meaning. Prose is the right medium for this modern
declaration of faith, just because we expect poetry.
Practically all great declarations of faith are expressed
in poetry. Poetry, by its familiarity, would have con-
cealed the meaning. Prose here means what the whole
play means, that faith is a common thing, that everybody has a faith and lives by it. Mary and Joan speak
the same language, as they should for this play. It is
such speech as anyone might use if anyone today spoke
with visions. Yet it has a beautiful cadence. Doubtless
it could be written as free verse and would be found to

be good free verse. But it is better as it is. Its directness
and simplicity are exactly suited to the Maid.

Joan.

(*Kneeling*)

King of Heaven, the night is over. My jailors have worn themselves out with tormenting me, and have gone to sleep. And I
should sleep—I could sleep safely now—but the bishop's questions
come back to me over and over. What if I were wrong? How do
I know that my visions were good? I stare wide awake at the
dawn in the window and I cannot find an answer.—So many
things they said were true. It is true that the king we crowned
at Rheims is not wise nor just nor honest. It is true that his realm
is not well governed. It is true that I am alone, that my friends
have forgotten me, both the king and the nobles who fought
beside me. There is no word from them, no offer of ransom. And
I am doubly alone, for I have denied my visions, and they will
come to me no more.—I believe my visions to be good. I know
them to be good, but I do not know how to defend them. When
I am brought into a court, and must prove what I believe, how
can I prove that they are good and not evil?—Yes, and I ask
myself whether I have been honest always, for when I went
among men I acted a part. It was not only that I wore boy's
clothes.—I stood as my brother stood and spoke heartily as he
spoke, and put my challenges in the words he would have
spoken. When I spoke with my own voice nobody listened, nobody heard me, yet, was it honest to assume ways that were not
my own?—I know there's to be no answer. I can expect no
answer now, after I have betrayed and denied my saints.—They
will not burn me now because I admitted that I could not prove
my voices good—and I submitted to the church. And now, when
I am to live, when I have done what they say is right, I am more
unhappy than when they said I was wrong, and must die.[11]

Then her Voices speak to her again reassuringly. She has not done wrong. What she has done will set France free. She need not go to the fire if that is too difficult. Even so, she has done well.

Joan. You have spoken to me, and I denied you.

St. Michael. How would you understand these things, Jeannette? They confuse you with questions, questions that no man can answer. But the church itself is built on revelations, and these revelations came out of darkness and went back into darkness like your own.

Joan. They say I can prove nothing.

St. Michael. They can prove no more. In all the articles of belief and creed not one is capable of proof.[12]

When the churchmen come Joan tells them, "I have an answer now." Mary interrupts to say that now she has the answer too. Joan would compromise in little things, but not her beliefs, not her own soul.

It is not clear where she got that answer. Joan has not knowingly compromised at any point, though she has humbly admitted and deeply mourned her lack of understanding. But one thing Mary does know.

Mary. ... It doesn't matter what we try to say about her. Nobody can use her for an alien purpose. Her own meaning will always come through, and all the rest will be forgotten.

And her meaning does come through, despite the efforts of Masters and Mary to impose their meanings on her or find their meanings in her.

Joan. I have an answer now. I believe in them in my heart. There is no other authority.

Cauchon. Do you deny the authority of the church?

Joan. I believe in the church from my heart. There's no other way to believe.

Cauchon. The church has called your Voices evil. One or the other you must deny.

Joan. That's your belief, Bishop Cauchon, but not mine. Each must believe for himself. Each soul chooses for itself. No other can choose for it. In all the world there is no authority for anyone save his own soul.

Inquisitor. Then you choose death.

Joan. I know you have tried to save me.

Inquisitor. I have never tried to save you. I have spoken only for the strict and correct application of the canon law. When the law is on your side, I am there also. When you set yourself against the law I must set myself against you. But I still plead with you: do not force us to abandon you. The individual soul cannot choose its own faith, cannot judge for itself!

Joan. Yet every soul chooses for itself. Who chose your faith for you? Didn't you choose it? Don't you choose to keep it now?

Courcelles. There's a singular logic in this.

Cauchon. I think not.

Joan. Yes, you did choose it. You choose to keep it. As I choose to keep mine. And, if I give my life for that choice, I know this too now: Every man gives his life for what he believes. Every woman gives her life for what she believes. Sometimes people believe in little or nothing, nevertheless they give up their lives to that little or nothing. One life is all we have, and we live it as we believe in living it, and then it's gone. But to surrender what you are, and live without belief—that's more terrible than dying—more terrible than dying young.[13]

This is not only Joan's meaning, it is also Mr. Anderson's. Whether it is a tragic meaning may appear to be somewhat doubtful. The note of victory is too strong for the conventional view of tragedy. Joan has been guilty of no grievous error which has brought about her death. To be sure, the critic has no right to demand that Mr. Anderson shall write tragedies if he does not have a tragic view of life. The question arises because he appears to believe that he does have the tragic view. But when he is identifying himself with the tragedians he is limiting his definition of tragedy to the revelation of the truth that man is greater than his sufferings, that the dignity and significance of human life consists in the power to suffer. His serious plays, including *Joan of Lorraine*, answer to this description. But there has been a shift in emphasis from the overpowering sense of the evil which envelops man to the spirit of acceptance with which he meets his ruin. Mr. Anderson's hero sees so clearly that a man must die for what he believes or face the more terrible death of believing nothing, that the question of whether or to what extent he may have participated in the evil which engulfs him is reduced in force to such a degree as almost to eliminate the element of terror from the effect of the drama.

So powerful has been the influence of Greek tragedy and of Aristotle's definition of it on all subsequent drama that few writers have taken any account of the fact

that the difference in religion between the Greeks and
the moderns must produce some difference in modern
theatrical art. That difference is obvious in the plays of
Maxwell Anderson, who, of all modern playwrights, is
most keenly aware of the close relationship between
the religion of a people and their theatre. Despite his
protestation that he has never been a professing Christian, his plays end on a note of affirmation which is
not the traditional tragic tone. What he should have
discovered from his re-examination of the Sermon on
the Mount is that a Christian is identified not by his
professions but by his fruits. All of Mr. Anderson's
fruits are on the side of hope and faith. Perhaps he has
invented a new kind of drama. If the form he has
created for the embodiment of his vision of the dignity
and significance of human life does not correspond to
established forms, that is only to say that he is more
original than he is generally acknowledged to be.

[1] Maxwell Anderson, *Off Broadway*, William Sloane Associates, Inc.,
New York, 1947, pp. 61-62.
[2] ——, *Joan of Lorraine*, Anderson House, Washington, D. C., 1946,
Act I, Prologue, p. 8.
[3] *Ibid.*, Act I, Interlude IV, p. 80.
[4] *Ibid.*, Act I, Interlude II, p. 35.
[5] *Ibid.*, p. 50.
[6] *Ibid.*, Act II, Rehearsal Preface, p. 92.
[7] ——, *Off Broadway*, p. 11.
[8] ——, *Joan of Lorraine*, Act II, Rehearsal Preface, pp. 101-102.
[9] *Ibid.*, pp. 105-106.
[10] *Ibid.*, Act II, Interlude II, pp. 121-122.
[11] *Ibid.*, pp. 126-127.
[12] *Ibid.*, pp. 127-128.
[13] *Ibid.*, Interlude III, pp. 135-136.

CHAPTER X

The Essence
of Tragedy

On first thought there would seem to be no justification for considering together two plays having so little in common as *Bad Seed* and *Lost in the Stars*—except the fact that these two remain to be considered. Yet, for our understanding of the works of so conscious an artist as Maxwell Anderson, there is as much meaning—though not the same meaning—in the contrast between these two plays as in that between *Second Overture* and *The Feast of Ortolans*. The difference between *Bad Seed* and *Lost in the Stars* is the difference between that view of tragedy in which evil is regarded as the ultimate power in the universe, and man, however heroic his struggle, is doomed to defeat; and the view that man learns by suffering, and though he may die in the learning he is not defeated.

Superficially the only thing the plays have in common is that Mr. Anderson did not invent the stories. Both are dramatizations of novels. *Bad Seed* is an adaptation of *The Bad Seed* by William March; *Lost in the Stars*, of *Cry, the Beloved Country* by Alan Paton. "If the works of the great poets teach anything," said James Russell Lowell in vindication of the borrowings of such writers as Chaucer and Shakespeare, "it is to hold mere invention somewhat cheap. It is not the finding of a thing but the making something out of it after it is found that is of consequence." What Mr. Anderson was able to make for the theatre out of the novels of William March and Alan Paton illustrates once more the remarkable versatility of this playwright. In *The Bad Seed* he found, what Shakespeare often found, a good story spoiled in the telling by its first author. The changes Mr. Anderson made in reclaiming the story, though few, are subtle and of the utmost importance. In the dramatic version, the characters are more appealing and more convincing, the story is more moving, the meaning is more credible. Mr. Anderson had, in *Cry, the Beloved Country*, a first-rate novel to work from; and the play, while it is not better than the novel —it had no need to be—is a new work with a meaning of its own.

Bad Seed is the story of a child criminal, based on the idea that a disposition to criminal behavior is hereditary. Rhoda Penmark, at the age of eight, has committed one murder; and she commits two more in the course of the play's action.

She is a bright, pretty, winsome youngster, who has some unusual traits which perplex her mother and her teachers but which merely add to her attractiveness for other people. She is a perfectionist. Whatever she does, she does extremely well. Nevertheless, she has failed to win the gold medal for penmanship at school. Claude Daigle, a shy, awkward, frail boy, whom she despises, won the medal; and Rhoda is resentful. She is convinced it should have been hers. At a school picnic she tries to take the medal away from Claude, and in the scuffle she pushes him off the wharf and he drowns. He could have recovered himself, for he was a good swimmer; but she hit him on the face and hands with one of her shoes which had iron cleats on them.

She is getting away with this killing rather nicely when her mother, Christine, discovers the missing gold medal in a drawer where Rhoda keeps her treasures. Christine has just learned from the head of the school that Rhoda had been seen on the wharf with Claude just before the accident. Christine questions Rhoda. The child tries to divert her mother by being very charming and affectionate, but her mother knows she is not really an affectionate child and that she puts on a good act in order to get what she wants. When the charm act fails, Rhoda lies—quite ingeniously. Christine is not taken in. She rebukes Rhoda sharply and persists in questioning her.

Rhoda is not shaken by her mother's probing, but she is beginning to be upset by the janitor, Leroy. He is tormenting her by pretending to know all about what she has done. He claims to recognize in her a kindred spirit.

Leroy. You want to know how I know how mean your are? Because I'm mean. I'm smart and I'm mean. And you're smart and you're mean, and I never get caught and you never get caught.[1]

Rhoda increases her mother's suspicion by trying to verify some of the stories about police methods with which Leroy has been trying to frighten her.

Christine's husband is away on a business trip. She has phoned her father and asked him to come to see her, not telling him of her real anxiety but only that she is lonely and troubled by an old dream she used to have as a child. She now decides to try to get information about criminal behavior from a friend, Reginald Tasker, who writes detective stories. She invites him to dinner, and questions him on the pretext of being interested in writing a mystery story herself.

Tasker is delighted to learn that Christine is expecting her father. Richard Bravo was formerly a very well-known crime reporter and Tasker has always wanted to meet him.

Christine comes quickly to the question which most concerns her: Do children ever commit murder, or is crime something that is learned?

Tasker assures her that children do commit real crimes, that there are people who seem to have been born with something like a genius for crime.

At this point Bravo arrives; and, after the introduction and exchange of civilities, he joins in the discussion. He contends that criminal children are always the result of environment.

Tasker disputes the point. Friends of his—doctors—

have told him that too much emphasis has been put upon environment, too little upon heredity.

Tasker. . . . They say there's a type of criminal born with no capacity for remorse or guilt—born with the kind of brain that may have been normal among humans fifty thousand years ago—...[2]

Bravo refuses to accept such testimony, and Tasker admits that the experts cannot prove their claims.

Tasker. They can't prove it, but they think there are such people. They say there are children born into the best families, with every advantage of education and discipline—that never acquire any moral scruples. It's as if they were born blind—you can't expect to teach them to see.

Christine. And do they look—like brutes?

Bravo. Are you sold on this?

Christine. I want to find out.

Tasker. Sometimes they do. But often they present a more convincing picture of virtue than normal folks. A wax rosebud or a plastic peach can look more perfect than the real thing. They imitate humanity beautifully.

Christine. But that's—horrible.

Tasker. Some of them seem to have done some pretty horrible things and kept on looking innocent and sweet.

Bravo. I'd like to examine the evidence. Not much sense discussing it till we do.

Tasker. Well, this clinic I frequent came long ago to the conclusion that there are bad seeds—just plain bad from the beginning, and nothing can change them.[3]

Tasker mentions Bessie Denker as a case in point.
She began in early childhood. He tries to get Bravo,
who covered the case for his newspaper, to tell the
story; but Bravo professes to have forgotten all about it.
It is evident that Bravo is trying to change the subject;
but Christine insists on hearing about Bessie Denker,
so Tasker tells what he can recall of the story. Bessie
Denker poisoned her victims; and she finally disap-
peared, leaving no trail which the police could follow.
Tasker thinks there was a child—a little girl. Bravo
never heard of a child.

After Tasker leaves, Christine goes on questioning
her father until she breaks through his guard.

"It cannot be inherited! It cannot!" he exclaims in
great agitation.

Christine then promises that she will ask no more
questions; but she adds, after a pause, "Only I have
the answer now."

Her father tries to reassure her by telling her what
she has meant to him.

Christine. You found me somewhere.

Bravo. Yes. In a very strange place—in a strange way.

Christine. I know the place.

Bravo. I don't think you could. You were less than two years old.[4]

But she does remember the place, and she recalls

the name she heard her mother calling on that terrible night.

Bravo then tells her he was covering the case for a Chicago paper. He wired his wife to join him. They could not resist the lovely child who had eluded her mother's vicious purpose.

Christine cries out in anguish: Why wasn't she left there to die?

Bravo. There are places and events in every man's life he'd rather not remember. Don't let it hurt you now. It's past and doesn't touch you.

Christine. I wish I had died then! I wish it! I wish it!

Bravo. It hasn't mattered where you came from! You've been sound and sweet and loving! You've given me more than I ever gave or could ever repay! If you'd been my own I couldn't have hoped for more! You knew nothing but love and kindness and you've given love and kindness and sweetness all your life! Kenneth loves you, and you've made him happy. And Rhoda's a perfect, sweet, sound little girl!

Christine. Is she, father? Is she?

Bravo. What has she done?

Christine. She's—it's as if she were born blind!

Bravo. It cannot happen! It does not happen![5]

Bravo is not able to remain long with Christine. When he is gone Christine notices that Rhoda is surreptitiously trying to get something wrapped in paper out of the apartment. She insists on seeing what it is, and finds it is the shoes with the cleats on them. Rhoda has not worn the shoes since the day of the picnic. Christine now realizes that Rhoda must have hit Claude with one of the shoes. Rhoda is a little fury in the struggle over the parcel, kicking and biting to protect her secret; but when her mother sees the shoes and guesses the truth, Rhoda tells her the whole story. Rhoda is genuinely frightened and begs her mother for comfort.

Rhoda. Mother, mother, please say you won't let them hurt me! Please!

Christine. (*Putting her arms around Rhoda*) Nobody will hurt you. I don't know what must be done now, but I promise you nobody will hurt you.[6]

While Christine is trying to resolve her problem Leroy goes on tormenting the child whenever he finds her alone. He tricks her into admitting that she hit Claude with her shoe; but she tells him the police will never find the shoes because she has burned them. Leroy says he found the shoes in the incinerator and took them out. That frightens her, and she demands that he return the shoes to her. Her manner, so cold but so insistent, alarms him. He tries to retreat. He tells her he was only teasing. But he has pushed his luck too far. She knows that he is in the habit of napping on a bed of excelsior which he has made for himself in the garage. She watches until she finds him asleep, sets fire to the excelsior, locks the garage door, and lets him burn to death. While the entire neighborhood goes into a panic, she goes into the den and plays the piano.

Christine, who saw Rhoda take matches from the kitchen, realizes what has happened. She collapses in hysteria momentarily, but does not reveal her knowledge of the child's crime to the friend who hovers over her.

Christine. Don't let me get my hands on her.

Monica. Christine, she's only a child.

Christine. You didn't see it! You could look away and play the piano, but it happened!

Monica. Christine. Please be sensible. What has she done?

Christine. It's not what she's done—it's what I've done.[7]

Christine recovers quickly, and by evening she has made her decision. When Rhoda is lying on the couch ready for bed Christine tells her that she has some new vitamins for her to take, and she gives Rhoda a lethal dose of sleeping pills. Rhoda tells her mother what Leroy has been saying to her, and once more begs her mother, "Don't let them hurt me, Mommy."

When the child has fallen asleep Christine speaks to herself in a brief soliloquy. She cannot let them take Rhoda away and shut her up. She picks up Rhoda and carries her to her bed. Then she returns and goes into the den, and a shot is heard.

In the last scene Kenneth Penmark and Monica are pondering the mystery of Christine's suicide, and Monica tries to comfort him with the blessed thought that Rhoda's life was saved.

Rhoda is playing the piano in the den. She comes in presently to ask sweetly if Daddy liked what she was playing. She was playing for him. Then seeing his depression she beguiles him with the little game they have always played.

Rhoda. I love you. Daddy! What will you give me for a basket of kisses?

Kenneth. For a basket of kisses? (*He looks at Rhoda*) Oh, my darling—I'll give you a basket of hugs! (*His arms go round her*)[8]

Bad Seed is one of Mr. Anderson's greatest achievements in the dramatization of an idea, in the sense that the meaning is completely expressed through character and action without any need of overt comment. There is only one place where the author intrudes to make his own observation, and it is quite inappropriate. Tasker's comment on the supremacy of evil repeats something which Elizabeth had said much better, because in her case it is spoken in the heat of passion.

Tasker. Sometimes I wonder whether these malignant brutes may not be the mutation that survives on this planet in this age. This age of technology and murder-for-empire. Maybe the softies will have to go, and the snake-hearted will inherit the earth.[9]

This is pathetically feeble by comparison with Elizabeth's astounding outcry, "The rats inherit the earth!"

Bravo's rejoinder is not even pertinent: "I'm betting on the democracies." What are we to suppose democracy could do to alter the facts of life, if it is a fact that persons may be born morally blind? Dialogue such as this can do nothing to heighten, can only detract from, the perfect tragic effect of the last scene of the play. No sensitive reader or playgoer could miss the appalling significance of Rhoda's surviving her mother.

William March depended for his effects on accentuating the morbid elements, the gruesome details, the unattractive traits of the child murderess. His Rhoda is cold, resistive, obvious in her acquisitiveness, so lacking in affection as to be hardly attractive even to her mother. Mr. Anderson's Rhoda is pretty, utterly charming in her quaint way, disarmingly frank in her acquisitiveness, merely unresponsive to demonstrations of affection, convincing when she puts on an act for any purpose, in every way a little more truly human. Far from lessening the effect of horror, the more appealing personality of the child heightens that effect.

The modulation of Christine's character is equally subtle and equally effective. In Mr. Anderson's telling of the story Christine is appalled by her child's behavior, but there is almost nothing of the feeling of revulsion which mars her character in the novel. Except in moments of surprise, when she is provoked to exasperation, her feeling is one of compassion for the child. There is little compassion in her nature as she was originally conceived. In the novel her anxiety is self-centered.

There are important changes in the action also. Christine's stark, lonely, morbid struggle with her problem in the novel is alleviated by bringing her father into the action. He focuses attention on her personal loveliness, thereby accentuating the poignancy of her situation. And of course his presence speeds up the resolution of the plot.

Nothing could be more clumsy than the method by which William March handles Christine's solution of her problem by having a total stranger at the public library suggest an ending for the hypothetical crime story. Mr. Anderson's transfer of that role to Tasker, a personal friend, is infinitely better. And such gruesome details as Christine's lingering over hideous newspaper pictures of her mother in the electric chair are entirely eliminated.

Bad Seed is a thoroughly absorbing drama, and any dispute as to the truth or falsity of the basic idea is quite beside the point. Christine is just the sort of person who would easily believe Tasker's explanation: It is like being born blind. The image itself is compelling. Moreover, it is not an incredible theory that all tragedy may be the result of ignorance. Even if the scientific fact could have been established, that would not have altered the problem for Christine. What she could not face was that her child, her baby whom she loved, should be turned over to institutional care. Something drastic had to be done. Given the persons and the situation, a tragic outcome was inevitable.

Lost in the Stars affords one of the best illustrations of what Mr. Anderson specifies as the function of prophecy in art—providing visions of idealized life which operate as direct motivation to more enlightened conduct.

Stephen Kumalo, a Zulu Christian pastor, has left his little home in Ndotsheni to go to Johannesburg, ostensibly to rescue his erring sister Gertrude, whose conduct is offending their brother John, but really to try to find his own son Absalom, who went to Johannesburg more than a year ago to earn money for his education. At the railway station, as he was leaving, he encountered the Jarvises—father, son, and grandson. The son, Arthur, greeted Stephen and his wife in open cordiality. James Jarvis, the father, was deeply incensed.

Jarvis. If you had struck me across the face you couldn't have hurt me more—or damaged me more, in the eyes of those who stand here. I suppose you know that?

Arthur's only answer is,

I have friends among the Zulus. And my friends are my friends.[10]

His father is not sure, then, that he wants Arthur to visit him again.

In Johannesburg Stephen learns from his brother that Absalom left the mines and went about with John's son Matthew. Stephen is sent from one person to another until he arrives at the parole office, where the officer, Mark Eland, tells him that the boys were stealing and Absalom has been in jail. He is now paroled to Eland, is working in a factory, and is living with a pregnant girl in Shanty Town. Eland promises to take Stephen to see him in the morning.

Meanwhile, at a dive in Shanty Town, Absalom, Matthew, and another youth, Johannes, are planning to burglarize the home of Arthur Jarvis. Johannes, who formerly worked in Arthur's home, tells the others that the doors are never locked, because Arthur Jarvis has some kind of theory. Matthew is insisting that Absolom must bring his gun. Absalom is unwilling. Why should he have a gun if the house is not locked and they do not expect anyone to be there? But Matthew is adamant.

Matthew and Johannes leave, and Irina, Absalom's girl, comes looking for him. She says the parole officer has been at their hut and that she told him Absalom was at work. The officer is coming again. Irina begs Absalom to come home. He says he is going away where he will never be found. He is going to the new gold fields for he loves her, and wishes to give her a better life. She is afraid and begs him to come home. He has just agreed to go with her when Matthew returns and taunts him. He sends Irina away and leaves with the boys to attempt the burglary.

The next morning Eland takes Stephen to Irina's hut in Shanty Town. Absalom is not there. They will go to the factory; he is there, of course. Irina then tells the officer that Absalom is not at work, that she has been lying to him. Then Stephen asks Eland to let him speak to her alone.

He tests her, trying to discover whether she is really in love with Absalom. Satisfied that she is, he leaves her for the time being. When he has gone she sings a wistful love song revealing the sincerity of her passion. The poetic quality of her nature reminds one of Oparre, though the two women are quite different in most respects. The similarity is the more remarkable in that

Maxwell Anderson did not have Alan Paton's authentic models to work from in creating Oparre.

The robbery did not proceed as planned. The boys were surprised to find a servant in the house; and when the servant cried out Arthur Jarvis appeared. Absalom shot and killed Arthur.

When James Jarvis and Mark Eland talk about the murder, Jarvis has already begun to be affected by his son's point of view. He is still severe, insisting that there is only one way to deal with the blacks. They understand and respect nothing but firm discipline. But he is shaken.

Jarvis. I differed sharply with my son concerning our policy toward the blacks, but in this I want what he would have wanted —that the guilty feel the penalty—no man else.[11]

Eland says Arthur will be a great loss. As a parole officer he would have given up many times but for Arthur.

Jarvis. And yet they killed him. What would he have said about a crime like this?

Eland. He would have said, "They live in such poverty and fear. They see no way out of their poverty or their fear and they grow desperate."[12]

When Stephen sees his son he assures Absalom of his faith in him, that he knows Absalom could not have committed the crime. But Absalom confesses and names the two others. He says he did not mean to kill. They had thought Arthur Jarvis would not be at home; they were surprised.

In the last scene of Act I Stephen, in his grief, is trying to write the news to his wife. The act closes with the title song, "Lost in the Stars."

This is an old theme with Mr. Anderson, a theme that goes all the way back to the little book of poems published at the begining of his writing career. Only a virtuoso could have achieved such variations upon a single theme, making it express his own youthful skepticism, the cynicism of Mio in *Winterset,* the faith of D'Alcala in *Key Largo,* and the sorrowing perplexity of a Christian minister in this play. The son has dramatic validity here, for it forecasts the profound sense of lostness with which Stephen confronts his congregation near the end of Act II and gives symmetry to the structure of the play. Act II opens in John's tobacco shop. John is getting a good lawyer for the boys, a white man's lawyer, who will defend all three. Stephen says Absalom will plead guilty, because he is guilty. John tries to explain to Stephen: "It's a game. Truth has nothing to do with it."

Stephen wrestles with his problem. How shall he counsel his son? Must he urge Absalom to speak the truth although it will probably cost him his life? Or shall he, a minister of Christ, consent to the boy's attempt to save his life by lying? At last he goes to James Jarvis and begs him to intercede.

Stephen. If I could take him back to his home, umnumzana! Away from Johannesburg. He grew up in Ndotsheni. Among the hills. There was no evil in him then. From our house we could see up through the clove to your great house. You were kind to the folk who worked the little farms. Be kind again. A terrible thing has befallen my people. We are lost. Not many have found their way to the Christ, and those who have not are lost. My son was lost. This would not have happened if there were not the gold mines, and the great city your people have built, and the little hope we have.

Jarvis. Umfundisi, there are two races in South Africa. One is capable of mastery and self-control—the other is not. One is born to govern, the other to be governed. One is capable of culture and the arts of civilization—the other is not. The difference between us is greater than that I live on a hill and you live in the valley. If my son had killed your son I would not have come to you for mercy. Nor to the judge. Whether it were my son or yours, I would have said, let him answer the law![13]

Absalom pleads guilty and is sentenced to hang. The other two boys are acquitted. In the prison afterwards Absalom and Irina are married, and Stephen promises to take Irina with him to Ndotsheni and care for the child as his own. Absalom thanks him with dignity. Stephen tells him there will be an appeal, but Stephen has no hope in it. Absalom admits his fear of the hanging. He has his father's simplicity.

Stephen takes Gertrude's son Alex, as well as Irina, and returns to Ndotsheni.

Almost immediately Alex and Edward Jarvis discover one another. James Jarvis finds the boys together in the little church and rebukes his grandson for fraternizing with Zulus. Edward protests, and his grandfather sinks down on the steps of the church, his head in his hands. This is Arthur and Stephen beginning all over again. He does not know why children should obey,

or whether good or evil comes of it. But there are some
things he cannot bear to look upon.

While he is sitting there Stephen and his wife and
the people come into the church. Stephen speaks to the
people. He tells them his son is to die on the scaffold,
and that he is resigning.

Stephen. .... The man he killed was known to you, too. He was
Arthur Jarvis. He was born in the hills above our little town.
There was a brightness upon him even as a child. As a man he
was a friend of our race, a friend of all men, a man all men could
be proud of. And my son—killed him. And the mother of Arthur
Jarvis is dead of grief for her son. My people, if I stay here now
I become a hindrance to you, and not a help. I must go.[14]

The people protest. But Stephen reminds them that
their village is poor. In the past Arthur Jarvis has helped
them. He will not help them again; and no one will help
them while Stephen remains.

Stephen. I must go for still another reason, my dear people.
When I began to serve my God and my church I had a sure
faith that the God of our world ordered things well for men. I
had a sure faith that though there was good and evil I knew
which was good, and God knew it—and that men were better in
their hearts for choosing good and not evil. Something has shaken
this in me. I am not sure of my faith. I am lost. I am not sure now.
I am not sure that we are not all lost. And a leader should not
be lost. He should know the way, and so I resign my place.[15]

The congregation sings "A Bird of Passage."

This is the life of men on earth:
Out of darkness we come at birth

Into a lamplit room, and then—
Go forward into dark again.[16]

This hymn, from the little parable of the swallow from the oldest English history, is a very lovely thing. Mr. Anderson is not often successful with literary allusion. I have already commented upon the dubious choice of Dryden as a poet likely to be known to the persons in *The Star Wagon*. Similarly, Mio's astounding knowledge of the whole range of Western literature is highly improbable. On the other hand, the use of the Shakespeare sonnet in *Key Largo* is so probable as to be painfully trite. But this transfer of a bit of allegory from the beginning of Christianity in our own cultural past to a similar situation with which few of us would ever think of identifying ourselves is wonderfully imaginative.

The last scene of the play takes place in Stephen's house on the morning of the execution. The chorus sings "Why do they choose the morning?"

James Jarvis knocks at the door and asks to come in. Stephen is surprised. Jarvis says he was outside the church yesterday and heard what Stephen said to his people and what they said to him, and he wants Stephen to know that he will help with the church—the roof, the painting, whatever needs to be done—he will do whatever Arthur would have done.

Stephen thanks Mr. Jarvis, but looks at the clock and says it is hard to think of the church just now.

Jarvis. I know. I couldn't sleep—thinking of it.

Stephen. I think this does not touch you.

Jarvis. Yes. It does.

Stephen. I don't know how. I think it might be better if I sat here alone.

Jarvis. I know my presence pains you. I know I am the last man in the world you wish to see. And yet—may I stay for a moment?

Stephen. If you wish.

Jarvis. Stephen Kumalo, my wife is dead. My son is dead. I live in a house with a child who knows me only as an old man. I have thought many times I would be better dead. I thought myself alone in this desolation that used to be my home. But when I heard you yesterday I knew that your grief and mine were the same. I know now that of all the men who live near this great valley you are the one I would want for a friend. And— I have been walking about—and came and knocked here now— because I wanted to sit with you in this hour—

Stephen. You want to sit with me?

Jarvis. Yes, if I may.

Stephen. Mr. Jarvis, you know that you can give me only charity. If you were seen to touch my hand, this town, this whole valley, would turn against you.

Jarvis. I've finished with that. I haven't come here lightly. I shall take your hand whenever I like, before whom I like. I shall come and worship in your church if I wish to worship. May I sit here with you?

Stephen. Yes, umnumzana.[17]

Jarvis sits. Stephen says that he will have to give up his pastorate.

Stephen. If I stayed, do you know what I would preach here? That good can come from evil, and evil from good! That no man knows surely what is evil or what is good! That if there is a God He is hidden and has not spoken to men! That we are all lost here, black and white, rich and poor, the fools and the wise! Lost and hopeless and condemned on this rock that goes 'round the sun without meaning!

Jarvis. Not hopeless, Stephen, and not without meaning. For even out of the horror of this crime some things have come that are gain and not loss. My son's words to me and my understanding of my son. And your words in the chapel, and my understanding of those words—and your son's face in the courtroom when he said he would not lie any more or do any evil. I shall never forget that.

Stephen. You think well of my son?

Jarvis. I tried not to. But you and I have never had to face what Absalom faced there. A man can hardly do better than he did when he stood before the judge. Stay in Ndotsheni, Stephen, stay with those who cried out to you in the chapel. You have something to give them that nobody else can give them. And you can be proud of Absalom.

Stephen. And he is forgiven, and I am forgiven?

Jarvis. Let us forgive each other.

Stephen. Umnumzana—umnumzana!

Jarvis. Let us be neighbors. Let us be friends.[18]

This scene of reconciliation is Mr. Anderson's own creation. It is quite different from the corresponding scene in the novel when James Jarvis, on horseback, encounters Stephen going to his mountain vigil. What was almost naïvete in the novel is in the play the magnificent courage of complete honesty, the genuine humility of a great soul. Stephen's simple confession of lostness is language to redeem all the degradation which that great theme has suffered at the hands of street-corner evangelists. It is his faith, not his position of leadership, which sustains the shock in the play. All this may be less authentic South African sociology, but it is richer drama.

Lost in the Stars was a theatrical failure in 1949. The American people, for all their protestations to the contrary, are not yet ready to accord "Liberty and justice to all." It will take more than little boys ceremonially pledging allegiance to the flag to accomplish the needed reconciliation. Yet we are struggling toward that goal; and nothing can do more to help us forward than the visions of possibility provided by romantic art. The Broadway audience of 1949 will not have the last word, for all across the land young people have recordings of *Lost in the Stars*. They know and love the lyrics and the choruses. There will come a time when what was new has become a memory, a musical memory for a whole generation, freighted with the nostalgia for school and college days and the idealism of its youth. Then there will be a revival of *Lost in the Stars*, and Maxwell Anderson, who knows of no instance of a playwright's leaving works behind him to gain acceptance after the author has gone, may be the first. For the honor of a prophet is necessarily belated. Those who step out ahead to find and show us the way have always had to go it alone. The cry of loneliness which has echoed throughout the plays of Maxwell Anderson is in the playwright himself; but it is not a cry of despair. It is "the voice of one crying in the wilderness," crying the beloved country, the promised land, the new Jerusalem, the hope of mankind: "Let us be neighbors. Let us be friends."

[1] Maxwell Anderson, *Bad Seed*, Dodd, Mead and Company, New York, 1955, p. 51.

[2] *Ibid.*, p. 58.

[3] *Ibid.*, pp. 58-59.

[4] *Ibid.*, p. 66.

[5] *Ibid.*, p. 67.

[6] *Ibid.*, p. 71.

[7] *Ibid.*, p. 88.

[8] *Ibid.*, p. 96.

[9] *Ibid.*, p. 61.

[10] ——, *Lost in the Stars*, William Sloan Associates, Inc., New York, 1950, pp. 10-11.

[11] *Ibid.*, p. 41.

[12] *Ibid.*, p. 42.

[13] *Ibid.*, p. 60.

[14] *Ibid.*, p. 79.

[15] *Ibid.*, p. 80.

[16] *Ibid.*, p. 81.

[17] *Ibid.*, p. 84.

[18] *Ibid.*, p. 85.

Index

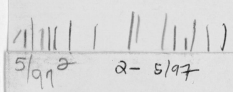

5/97²   2 - 5/97